Seven Pillars

Seven Pillars

What Really Causes Instability in the Middle East?

Essays by
Danielle Pletka • Michael Rubin
A. Kadir Yildirim • Thanassis Cambanis
Florence Gaub • Michael A. Fahy
Bilal Wahab • Brian Katulis

Edited by Michael Rubin and Brian Katulis

THE AEI PRESS

Publisher for the American Enterprise Institute
WASHINGTON, DC

ISBN-13: 978-978-0-8447-5024-8 (Hardback)
ISBN-13: 978-0-8447-5025-5 (Paperback)
ISBN-13: 978-0-8447-5026-2 (eBook)

American Enterprise Institute
1789 Massachusetts Avenue, NW
Washington, DC 20036
www.aei.org

Contents

What Really Causes Instability in the Middle East?

DANIELLE PLETKA

Writing in the wake of the September 11, 2001, terror attacks, the late historian Bernard Lewis famously asked, "What Went Wrong?" as he and others attempted to explain how a region that was once a beacon for civilization and science had descended into such radicalism and anger.[1] Students, journalists, and policymakers can debate his and now thousands of other treatises on the malaise of the modern Middle East, but the validity of the question itself is beyond doubt. War, dictatorship, human misery, poverty, extremism, regression, and one foreign intervention after another are the modern tale of a world that was once at the pinnacle of human accomplishment. What went wrong indeed?

Too many areas of modern study are subject to the vagaries of fashion and theory, and the Arab world and Iran are not immune. Scholars of the Middle East have for decades tried to find the magic formula to "repair" the region: If only dictatorships were more benign, some argued, while others sang the virtues of democratization. The key was tolerating Islamism, unless, of course, the true path to modernity rested in promoting Atatürk-style secularism. If economic reform should precede political liberalization, then would a splash of socialism be necessary to alleviate poverty, or is foreign direct investment the key? Diplomats have long argued the road to peace and stability runs through Jerusalem, unless of course it runs instead through Baghdad, Damascus, or Tehran. Pan-Arabism, Gulf cooperation, women's rights, and sundry other often contradictory panaceas could well soothe the ills that ail the Middle East. Each new theory or conclusion had one thing in common: The best laid plans could not trump reality. Scholars, policymakers, and military leaders, whether in the region or outside, have all too often been wrong.

With habits of mind like Marxist ideologues, some academics and policy practitioners lament that favored solutions do not work because they have not been faithfully implemented. Perhaps. Others prefer to quibble over semantics, forever arguing about how the Middle East should be defined and what modernity is. But it is also true that many good analysts are all too ready to deny the Middle East's residents the agency they deserve. It is easy to hang the region's ills on colonialism and borders, but sectarian divisions ebbed and flowed over the centuries. Social tensions, political instability, and economic woes all predate the coming of the Western armies or, for that matter, diplomats. Only one thing cannot be denied: It is quite a mess. But why?

While diplomats and politicians regularly propose a cure, they often fail to consider what causes the disease. At its core, what drives the instability of the modern Middle East? Platitudes about the ills of colonialism or the lack of a reformation within Islam are simply the latest fashions imposing themselves on what passes for trenchant analysis.

At a series of dinners early in the process of assembling this work, a large and diverse group of scholars of the Middle East came together in pursuit of answers. They came from a variety of disciplines: history, political science, anthropology, religious studies, and economics. And a variety of professional backgrounds: military and intelligence professionals, diplomats, journalists, and aid workers. Some served in Democratic administrations, and others in Republican ones. Surprisingly, even though many had studied the same region for decades, the artificial walls between academe and policy on the one hand and liberals and conservatives on the other meant that many had never before met, let alone sat over a dinner to discuss and debate fundamental perceptions. The challenge was straightforward: to tease out fundamental pillars of instability that affect the Middle East.

Indeed, while the so-called Arab Spring might have garnered headlines, and events in Egypt, Libya, Syria, and Yemen recriminations, the simple fact is the revolutions that began in 2011 are more symptoms of the afflictions that plague the region than driving forces. We identified seven such pillars, as much a play on T. E. Lawrence's *Seven Pillars of Wisdom* as an attempt to drive home that these "pillars" are the long poles in the tent of Middle Eastern turmoil.

Legitimacy

In Michael Rubin's contribution, he peels away the oft-relied-upon trope about the illegitimacy of the modern Middle East, the hard to prove but all too often blindly accepted notion that colonialism and arbitrary borders have been the true force behind the many coups and ructions that have shaken governments across the Middle East and North Africa. Yet it is true that there is a crisis of legitimacy in the Arab world and Iran: "Historically," Rubin explains, "questions about legitimacy do more to spark revolution than poverty or resistance against tyranny."

The missing element in most cases is the most obvious source of legitimacy for any leader: the consent of the governed. As a result, leaders for decades have looked to alternative sources of legitimacy, religion being the most frequent refuge for those in search of a modicum of acceptance by their people. Almost all the region's constitutions look to Islam as a source of legitimacy. Others go further, some with nuance, such as the Islamic Republic of Iran, and others without, such as the Islamic State. Similarly, religious sectarian representation—most crudely designed in Lebanon's national charter but also informally applied in Iraq—has become a force behind claims of legitimacy or lack thereof. Yet, even as religion becomes a crutch for those seeking legitimacy, many of these regimes lean on it at their own peril, lest they corrupt religion in the eyes of the people.

Perhaps effectiveness then is the true source of legitimacy? Not necessarily, according to Rubin. After all, monarchies in the region have proved a certain resilience, even as they have been, to varying degrees, deeply ineffective managers and custodians of power. And then again, citizens have often proved they will choose sectarian loyalty over effective leadership, undercutting the notion that good government is what can buy legitimacy. Ultimately, resilient institutions can provide the magic sauce that earns a leader legitimacy. But the road map toward building those institutions is unclear at best.

Islam and Islamists

It has become vogue to lament the failure of a reformation within Islam as the source of both the failings of the Middle East and the draw of

Islamism. Egyptian President and strongman Abdel Fattah al Sisi said that it was necessary to "purge" religious discourse "of its flaws."[2] But as A. Kadir Yildirim explains, "Ultimately, the legitimacy of religious discourse as a viable public policy options rests on the *failure of secular policies*, not on the merits of religious discourse."

For many years, most regimes in the region paid little more than lip service to Islam, turning to it only as a last resort when all other sources of legitimacy failed. Saudi Arabia and Iran were the exceptions that proved the rule. Still, one cannot look at the Middle East, even understanding that Sunni-Shi'a rifts have become a proxy for a battle between Iran and its neighbors, and believe that religion plays no role.

But what is its role? Certainly, there are elements of faddishness. More and more women, not compelled to do so, have embraced the hijab. Islamist conservatism, while extricable from extremism, is gaining, not losing, popularity.

Islam, it is almost impossible to deny, has become a political last resort in the face of the failure of the many other experimental isms of the modern Middle East. And claimants to the mantle of Muhammad have themselves embraced a regressive and Salafi-jihadi-influenced creed. Still, "unless and until the Islamist critique of secular governance can be decoupled from its religious component," Yildirim concludes, "it is hard to imagine a socio-political context in which Islamic reform can be successfully debated."

Ideology

Almost wistfully, Thanassis Cambanis begins his consideration of the role of ideology in the Arab world noting that some believe the 21st century is a "post-ideological age," but that cannot in any circumstance be considered the case in the modern Middle East. This is, after all, a region that adores ideology; these are the isms that littered the 20th-century Arab world, milestones in a never-ending effort to restore past glories.

It is difficult to take seriously—at least politically—the creeds that come and go, part of elite efforts to "choreograph consent." Cambanis lays out an assortment of new ideologies that are making their way—resistance, mercantile monarchy, and militarism—some seeking to displace Islamism, but with little prospect for success. In too many cases, however, these are ex post facto descriptive terms for political problems and the status quo. The supreme leader in Iran has crafted the notion of an axis of resistance to underpin externally imposed sanctions and restrictions on the Iranian economy. Sisi has burnished his militarism as an antidote to the unsettling popularity of the Muslim Brotherhood at home. And so on.

Yet none of these ideologies, some sold with the ardor of a Madison Avenue pro across nationally owned satellite proxies and in the echo chambers of the region, offer any hope of evolution out of the turmoil that has plagued the Middle East. To the contrary, ideology, like Islam, is the pale substitute for systems and institutions that are the cornerstones of stability.

Cambanis also touches on the notion of culture and how evolving communications and media technology can both reinforce and rebuff ideology. Gamal Abdel Nasser had the radio, and Ayatollah Ruhollah Khomeini had the audio tape. How the cell phone, WhatsApp, and Telegram generation will leave a lasting impact on society is one of the fundamental questions with which both rulers and the ruled must now grapple.

Middle Eastern Militaries

Historically, Arab strongmen have relied on the notion of the military as an agent of stability to sell their appeal. The facts tell another story: Florence Gaub leads with the telling numbers. "Since 1932, the year of Iraqi independence, [military forces] have interfered in politics, attempting 73 coups across the region and succeeding in 39." Clearly, Arab militaries are not agents of long-term stability. But why?

The problem begins with the makeup of regional militaries. While conscription remains the rule in some of the region's nations, other factors are at play. Outside compulsion, the main reason for joining the military across the Middle East is economic. With unemployment rates among young men in the 25–30 percent realm even in richer economies, having something to do is a key driver for inscription.[3] That is not a recipe for success, particularly when pay scales are shockingly low everywhere outside the Gulf region.

Then there are the predilections of regional militaries: Quantity, and not quality, is the hallmark. In nations that spend substantial portions of their gross domestic product on the military (much of it on personnel), there is shockingly little bang for the buck. Israel exposed these deficiencies in 1948 and has continued doing so. More than seven decades later, Arab militaries are not notably improved.

Part of the reason is sectarianism in a variety of forms. In some cases, militaries have explicit quotas, such as in Lebanon. In others, such as Syria, a leader will seed the command with his sect to protect from coup plotters. In Iraq, Shi'ites were excluded under Saddam Hussein. Now the infamous Iraqi military, shed of that sectarian legacy, must compete with sectarian militias sponsored by outside powers. As in civil war–striven Lebanon of the 1970s and '80s, militias both challenge the regular military and draw talent away from its ranks. Still others discriminate against Islamists (Egypt).

Across the region, one failing stands out without regard to national borders: "The absence of stringent education and training programs is mirrored in the poor strategic thinking taking place in most military decision-making circles." Most Arab states have no national security strategy. Iran's exists only through inference. Similarly, the concept of civil-military relations or civilian control of the military is almost nonexistent. Military budgets are almost without exception not itemized, so parliaments, where they exist, cannot demand accountability.

In a region that knows war as well as any in the world, most militaries represent political risk, insufficient national security, shoddy means of employment, and a source of instability for the very nations they are tasked to defend. It is inescapable that the region's militaries are among the root causes of the Middle East's almost incessant and violent churn.

Education

Michael Fahy ends his chapter on education with another scholar's observation about the region: "Desires for the future . . . have typically been transformative rather than ameliorative; they have aimed to create a new world, not to improve the one people actually live in."

Education is key to almost everything: upward mobility, competition, employment, health, and so much more. But a historically poor education system that fails to emphasize critical thinking is now also an overstretched and underfunded education system, hampered not just by disinvestment and growing populations but by conflict, sectarianism, and lack of advanced technology. Fahy notes that, while there are national variations, research agrees on several key points: Higher education in the region is among the poorest globally; graduates are ill-equipped to meet their own national challenges, let alone those in the global economy; and "genuine educational reform cannot take place without addressing the long-standing sociopolitical structures and cultural norms in which educational systems are embedded."

In short, the Arab world cannot be reformed without reforming education, and education cannot be reformed without reforming the Arab world. Small wonder that change is slow in coming. Change is not impossible, but it requires the kind of commitment heretofore lacking among both locals and their allies abroad.

The Economy

The chicken-and-egg conundrum of the Middle East—Is the region struggling because of Islam or turning to Islam because of the struggle? Is the legitimacy deficit a cause of militarism or the reverse? Is the search for ideological constructs a cause or result of a lack of institutions?—makes most discussions of the region's economic challenges a secondary matter. Much of the analysis comes down to "Well, what can you expect?" Yet it need not be so, as relatively speaking, the region is rich. And that is half the problem.

As Bilal Wahab notes, oil wealth has enabled half the region to resist reform, and aid handouts have enabled the other half to do the same. Oil wealth has been a reason to rape and pillage (see Saddam Hussein's invasion of Kuwait) and a means of exporting extremism (Saudi Arabia and Iran). And whether rich or poor, corruption is endemic, a reason for violence, the root of loss of faith and legitimacy, and, by any standard, shocking. Wahab reports, 19 of 21 Arab states scored "very low" on Transparency International's Corruption Perceptions Index.

The state sectors in rich petro-states employ legions. The state sectors in poorer nations also employ legions. Women are notably absent from the workforce. STEM education is a low priority across the region. Rule of law is missing on the financial side (taxation, bankruptcy, and legal precedent are all foreign concepts), and crony capitalism erodes trust in markets. On the whole, it should have come as little surprise that the suicide of an overregulated, frustrated, and deeply impoverished fruit vendor in Tunisia could spark a series of revolutions that would upend the entire Middle East.

But there is hope; this is an area that lends itself to technocracy. And as even the richest of the Gulf contemplate a less petro-dependent world, the incentives are strong to build market systems that can employ and sustain the hundreds of millions across the region.

Governance

Perhaps it all comes down to this: Faulty governance is the byword of the Middle East. Unreformed republics, retrograde monarchies, military dictatorships, and terrorist substates form the bulk of governance models in the region. Efforts at transition and reform often stall, and where tyranny fails to stir opposition, outside powers have been all too willing to step in and do so. Nominally legitimate systems have failed to deliver consistent results or adhere to their own self-imposed norms. As Brian Katulis sums up early in his chapter on governance, "For all its faults in delivering prosperity or accountability, this model of a military and state-dominated economy presided over by a repressive government with nominal elections has been resilient."

Over the years, and emphatically after the US invasion of Iraq and the failed attempts to secure a lasting peace, federalism and fragmentation have become attractive concepts. To some outsiders, division along ethnic or sectarian lines like the former Yugoslavia promises a solution to perpetual conflict; domestically, local stakeholders embrace notions of autonomy, though all too often with exactly the same antidemocratic and corrupt tendencies at the local level. In Syria, too, the notion of bottom-up grown power given the successes of certain local and community councils in the face of conflict has added fuel to the fragmentation fire. But Katulis notes that decentralization is almost as fraught as overcentralization: Without national accountability and vertically integrated governance structures, there is authoritarian drift.

Finally, it becomes clear, even when analyzing the staying power of certain monarchies or the consultant-driven technocratic reforms in the Gulf, that like the problem of legitimacy, the challenge of resting power in the consent of the governed is a distant model for the region. Almost all forms of governance have been tried, except genuine democracy. And finally, it is right to ask whether, given the structural, economic, educational, and military barriers to institution building, there is enough of a foundation on which to rest a genuine, functioning democracy.

***

It might be that, upon digesting these deeply researched conclusions about the pillars of instability in the Middle East, a reader and policymaker will conclude that the region is without hope. And the answer to that lies in both morality and history: The developed world cannot be disinterested in the fate of hundreds of millions. Both Europe and the United States have learned to their detriment that ignored, the problems of the region do not stay in the region. Every American president has declared his to be the era in which interventions in the Middle East end. Every one has been wrong.

Finally, the lessons of history are rich with structural and cultural impediments to national reform and success. The nations of Europe were such a tale, as were those of East Asia. Change can happen, but it requires vision and commitment.

But the quest for magic formulas geared to US or European political calendars is quixotic. If change is going to come to the Middle East, there must be a realistic understanding of the barriers to that change and a clear-eyed mission to overcome those barriers once and for all.

Notes

1. Bernard Lewis, *What Went Wrong? The Clash Between Islam and Modernity in the Middle East* (New York: Harper Perennial, 2006).

2. Shahira Amin, "President Sisi's Promise of Religious Revolution Remains Unfulfilled," Egyptian Streets, July 5, 2016, https://egyptianstreets.com/2016/07/05/president-sisis-promise-of-religious-revolution-remains-unfulfilled/.

3. Andrew England, "Middle East Jobs Crisis Risks Fueling Unrest, IMF Warns," *Financial Times*, July 12, 2018, https://www.ft.com/content/3daf3d5a-8525-11e8-a29d-73e3d454535d.

1

What Defines Legitimacy in the Middle East and North Africa?

MICHAEL RUBIN

The 2011 Arab Spring protests rocked the Middle East and North Africa. Some of the region's longest-standing regimes collapsed in a matter of days. When Zine El Abidine Ben Ali fell, he had ruled Tunisia for 23 years. Hosni Mubarak had ruled Egypt for three decades and was unapologetically setting the stage for his son Gamal to succeed him, much as Syrian dictator Hafez al-Assad had maneuvered to allow his son Bashar to take over in Damascus upon his death. In Yemen, the winds of the Arab Spring swept away Ali Abdullah Saleh after 33 years. And in Libya, a popular uprising ended Muammar Qadhafi's 42-year domination.

Each of these deposed Arab leaders had won international recognition as legitimate rulers of their countries, even when they found themselves in the crosshairs of the West or each other. President Ronald Reagan called Qadhafi "the madman of the Middle East" and described him as part of "a new, international version of Murder Incorporated," but never ceased recognizing him as the leader of Libya.[1] Likewise, first President George W. Bush and then President Barack Obama condemned and sought to isolate Bashar al-Assad, but they continued to recognize the reality of Assad's presidency even as they sought to undermine it.

What led these leaders' regimes to falter or collapse so precipitously? Were these leaders ever legitimate in the eyes of their people? Or did they simply lose their legitimacy along the way?

Legitimacy is a tricky topic across the Middle East, if not the broader world. Its definition is often transitory and shifts across time and space. To bastardize the late Supreme Court Justice Potter Stewart's observation about pornography, legitimacy is hard to define, but we know it when we see it. How Arabs or Berbers in Morocco define the legitimacy of their rulers is different from how Iranians, Iraqis, Kurds, Lebanese, or Turks do.

Historical experience varies across the region. Middle Eastern countries have different colonial experiences: Some fell under British dominance, and others under French. Many Arab states were part of the Ottoman Empire, while the Turks never penetrated others. Some countries are monarchies, while others are republics, having overthrown their kings in the 1950s or, in the case of Yemen and Libya, the 1960s. Governance varies across the region and, with it, notions of legitimacy. Time also matters. Some countries—Egypt and Iran, for example—have histories that date back millennia. Others—Iraq and Syria, and, for that matter, Israel—are modern resurrections of premodern concepts. Still others—Kuwait and Qatar, for example—are essentially tribes with flags.

But while legitimacy is hard to define, maintaining it is essential to stability. The late University of Houston political scientist G. Hossein Razi observed that legitimacy explains why people are willing to sacrifice their wealth and lives to fight for or against a regime.[2] Indeed, historically, questions about legitimacy do more to spark revolution than poverty or resistance against tyranny.

Political scientists and theorists have long debated the concept of sovereignty. Definitions of legitimacy most often focus (1) on who exercises it, (2) on what basis they exercise it, and (3) to what end it is exercised. The 18th-century Scottish essayist David Hume in his famous 1739 *A Treatise of Human Nature* argued that legitimacy was rooted in the provision of public goods.

> Bridges are built; harbours open'd; ramparts raid'd; canals form'd; fleets equip'd; and armies disciplin'd; everywhere, by the care of government, which, tho' compos'd of men subject to all human infirmities, becomes, by one of the finest and most subtle inventions imaginable, a composition, that is, in some measure, exempted from all these infirmities.[3]

University of California philosophy professor David Copp, meanwhile, argued, "The traditional view is that the legitimacy of a state would consist in its subjects' having a moral obligation to obey its law."[4] He defined sovereignty as "the right to non-interference" but suggested that consent of the governed was not necessary for legitimacy.[5]

In scholarship, literature on legitimacy has traditionally focused on Western concepts about governments both providing security and services and fulfilling the social contract between the governing and those governed. Here, perception comes into play: When governments use force against citizens, does it conform to the shared values of society?[6] Governments can execute murderers and rapists and retain legitimacy by shooting rioters threatening to burn businesses. To fire on opposing rallies or burn the businesses of their opponents, however, erodes government legitimacy, even if it does not destroy it.

Is Legitimacy Inherent in Nation-States?

Does the source of legitimacy in the West or, for that matter, East Asia transfer to the Middle East and North Africa? Not necessarily. In the Middle East, quality and form of government, and the values and ideologies on which regimes base themselves, vary wildly. Many variables influence legitimacy, but there appears to be no guaranteed formula.

Consider nationalism. Both the American and French revolutions influenced the Western concept of nationalism beginning in the 18th century. Countries developed symbols of nationalism such as flags and anthems. Beginning in the 19th century, Western countries organized more around ethnicity than religion. German states, whether Catholic or Protestant, coalesced around a common language. Along the Italian peninsula, various states—some of which had centuries of history as distinct entities—coalesced into a greater whole, once again centered on ethnicity and language.

The evolution of the nation-state in the Middle East was, of course, quite different. While the Middle East was the seat of civilizations and empires dating back millennia, recent centuries have not been kind to the region. The Spanish and Portuguese conquests of the New World created an influx of gold and silver, which sparked inflation and eroded the wealth of Middle Eastern empires. The gunpowder empires—the Mughals, Ottomans, and Safavids—which dominated the region from the 13th through 17th centuries, fractured. Their fall did not occur in a vacuum.

In 1798, Napoleon shocked not only Egyptians but also broader Islam-dom when he led a French invasion of Egypt. In the decades and centuries that followed, almost every corner of the Middle East and North Africa fell under the direct influence of foreign powers. There were exceptions; Great Britain and Russia encroached on Iran but never formally colonized it. While European powers slowly peeled away the Ottoman Empire's Arab provinces, a process that began decades before the 1916 Sykes-Picot Agreement, Turkish military hero Mustafa Kemal Atatürk prevented European powers from colonizing Anatolia itself. Nor did any foreign power ever penetrate into the interior of Arabia.

While Muslims in the Middle East and North Africa were familiar with nation-states due to their proximity to Europe, the concept of a nation-state imposed on the Middle East by the Western order was in dissonance to Islam, which preached the unity of the Muslim people. That said, while Islamists might argue that the nation-state is alien to Islam because it contradicts Islam's insistence on the unity of the *ummah*, the Muslim people, the reality is that unity was an elusive concept, even in the first decades after the Prophet Muhammad.

As states coalesced, they often sought to retroactively imbue themselves with a historic identity to help create a coherent national identity. Long before Saddam Hussein, successive Iraqi governments grasped on archaeology to root Iraq's legitimacy in a Babylonian past, even though Iraq only emerged as a state in the aftermath of World War I.[7] Lebanon claimed descent from the Phoenicians, Syria from the Assyrians, and Uzbekistan claimed to be the successor state to that established by Amir Timur (1336–1405), known to the West as Tamerlane, centuries before. As Bahrainis sought to rebuff Iranian claims to their suzerainty, they seized on findings of a Danish archaeological expedition to claim to be the inheritor to the mysterious Dilmun Empire referred to in the *Epic of Gilgamesh* but otherwise shrouded in the fog of time.[8] Israel, of course, bases its legitimacy on thousands of years of Jewish history in Palestine.

Even if, at times, the embrace of national myths rests more on fiction than historical reality, it would be a mistake to dismiss the states of the Middle East today as simply artificial constructs. A handful, of course, are. There was no real historical precedent for Jordan, Kuwait, Qatar, or the United Arab Emirates; Jordan was purely a colonial construction, and most Gulf states are essentially tribal fiefdoms. Straight-line borders may denote artificial boundaries drawn up in a colonial conference room, but artificial borders are not necessarily arbitrary.

Across the Middle East, civilizations grew alongside coasts and rivers. The vast majority of Egypt's population straddled the Nile, its fertile delta, or its Mediterranean coast. How colonial powers drew Egypt's borders in the desert away from major population centers did not affect 99 percent of the population. The same held true with Iraq, whose great cities grew up along the Euphrates and Tigris Rivers and the fertile farmland in between. Unlike in Africa, where colonial powers created nation-states without regard to historic units, in the Middle East, historic units remained largely whole.

This does not mean there were not disputes. The partition of Palestine is one obvious one, but so too was the division of Greater Syria, albeit into units that, except for Jordan, had their own claims to be coherent and historic units. Sometimes the disputes occurred when two peoples or groups were lumped together in a single state. Kurds resent their division into four states, and, decades after its independence, fault lines still exist between Tripolitania, as western Libya is historically called, and Cyrenaica, as the region bordering Egypt was once known.

Only in Iran did the state truly develop looking inward. There were some coastal towns on the Persian Gulf and Caspian Sea, but the true heart of Iran was in the Persian plateau, shielded from enemies and outsiders by mountain chains and malarial swamps. When natives of the Middle East blame problems exclusively on the West and the colonial imposition of national borders, such borders often recognized existing legitimacies; they did not simply impose artificial boundaries without rhyme or reason.

Simply put, there was no magic formula to imbue these nation-states with legitimacy. Historic precedent is important, except when it is not. Ideology can drive purpose, but its failure—Arab nationalism in Egypt, Marxism in South Yemen, and Baathism in Iraq and Syria—can simply reinforce the contributions nationalism and religion make toward legitimacy. Money also matters: Qatar is both an artificial country and, because of its gas reserves, the wealthiest state by per capita income. Its citizens have every incentive to embrace Qatari distinctiveness if only to prevent any further division of its natural wealth.

Even the most artificial states can craft national identities with the passage of time. Across the Middle East and North Africa, citizens of various countries can spot Kuwaitis, Palestinians, and Qataris by appearance and accent and place them distinctly vis-à-vis their neighbors. Common history has sharpened identity. Palestinian nationalism arose against the backdrop of Zionism. Iraq's 1990 invasion of Kuwait reinforced the notion of Kuwait-ness, and the Arab Quartet's 2017 blockade of Qatar, however justified, reinforced a distinct Qatari identity.

But, even if countries are legitimate on the world stage, the Arab Spring shows that within borders, government legitimacy can evaporate quickly. The Arab Spring never challenged the legitimacy of Egypt, Tunisia, or even Syria as an entity; it merely raised questions about the legitimacy of the government holding the reins of power. To understand legitimacy, then, what matters is not only the state but its government as well.

Does Islam Bestow Legitimacy on Government?

Highlighting the importance of religion to legitimacy is the fact that the constitutions of every Middle Eastern and North African state except Israel and Turkey reference Islam. Even nominally secular or liberal Arab states— Algeria, Tunisia, and the United Arab Emirates, for example—acknowledge Islam in their primary documents. The Islamic State staked its claim to legitimacy in the idea that religion meant more than borders. Islamic State leaders may have miscalculated, but the fact that they attracted tens of thousands of foreign fighters from more than 100 countries shows their ideology resonated.

That religion forms a platform for state legitimacy, of course, is not a phenomena exclusive to the Middle East. Many Western states also went through a period in which religion was the basis for legitimacy. During the Renaissance and the Enlightenment, religion infused monarchy. Kings and queens rose or fell over the question of religion, especially as the split between Catholicism and Protestantism grew.

But Christianity also enabled a separation of religion and state to develop. Romans 13:1-7, "Render unto Caesar the things that are Caesar's and unto God the things that are God's," provided leaders an ability to separate religion from rule and ultimately led to a separation of church and state in majority Christian countries. Any remaining links between religion and state in the West are more the vestiges of history and tradition than important components of political legitimacy. When the church does intercede in government in Western countries, it more often revolves around the morality of specific policies—abortion, euthanasia, or perhaps the Iraq War—rather than the legitimacy of government itself. And, in almost every case, the government and even officials who are personally religious do not hesitate to ignore or criticize the church for its intercessions.

In majority Muslim countries, however, Islam created a sharply different evolution of constitutional thought. Islam, like all religions, of course influences not only political identity but also notions of justice and social contracts between rulers and ruled. Islam historically has not been uniform regarding questions about the legitimacy of government. Khajarites, "seceeders," the theological ancestors of the Ibadis living primarily in Oman, argued that Muslims should invest political legitimacy only in the most pious Muslim. They cited al-Hujarat ("The Chambers"), the 49th chapter of the Quran, which declared, "Verily the most honored of you before God is the most righteous of you."[9] In practice, this meant an African slave had just as much claim to leadership as the inheritor of a tribal mantle or the son of a sultan. Hereditary leadership was illegitimate unless the son was, after his father, the most pious in the community. In addition, if a ruler did not remain religiously pure, the population could depose him. In effect, this led to what Razi called "puritanical republicanism."[10]

Traditional Sunni clerics uphold legitimacy of rulers so long as they profess Islam and maintain order.[11] As this creates an ossified establishment religion, it also opens the door for populist, lay religious movements. This was a trend that the late historian Bernard Lewis observed when he spoke about the divergence between "establishment Islam" and "popular Islam."[12] Whenever the two diverge, instability results.[13] Because Sunnism lacks an established, consensus religious hierarchy, such religious populism has become an increasing problem as radicals lacking credentials earned through decades of study issue *fatwas* and other religious declarations. Scholars and more traditional theologians can dismiss them as illegitimate, but ultimately, religion is as much what its practitioners believe it to be as what theologians at any given time say it is.

That is one of the reasons why, despite outside attempts to dismiss the Islamic State as "neither Islamic nor a state," many of its followers believed it to be religiously legitimate.[14] That Abu Bakr al-Baghdadi's creation subsequently bragged about erasing the borders of the post-Sykes-Picot era simply underscored the idea, at least in his followers' minds, that modern nation-states and borders lacked the legitimacy that the traditional notion of the caliphate embodied. There was ample basis, however, to also conclude that religious legitimacy did not require a caliphate. Early-20th-century Egyptian Salafi thinker Ali 'Abdel Raziq argued that believers accepted Islam to fulfill God's covenant, but that did not necessitate any particular form of government.[15]

Traditional Shi'ism teaches that the Hidden Imam will return to earth to usher in a just, Islamic government. Until then, therefore, clerics should not wield direct power over government because government is unjust and not purely Islamic. This, however, did not equate to a separation of mosque and state or secular governance. Clerics might expect leaders to consult them for religious guidance before major decisions to ensure conformity to Islam, but they would act more as an informal supreme court rather than an institutionalized managerial class.[16]

While still a young cleric in Iran, Ruhollah Khomeini adhered to this more traditional Shi'ite separation doctrine. "We do not say the government must be in the hands of the *faqih* [jurisprudent]," he argued in 1943, "rather we say the government must be run in accordance with God's rule."[17] But, as the shah accelerated his modernization program in the early 1960s, Khomeini became a figurehead for opposition. In 1970, six years into his Iraqi exile, then-Ayatollah Khomeini delivered a series of lectures published the following year in a book, *Hukumat-i Islami* (*Islamic Government*), which outlined his concept of *vilayat-i faqih* ("guardianship of the jurisprudent"), in practice, the theocratic rule of clerics.[18]

While *Hukumat-i Islami* was a bit vague in its practicalities, Khomeini's subsequent declarations hinted at his ultimate goals. "How is it that now, when it is the turn of the present generation of religious scholars to speak out, we invest excuses and say that it is 'incompatible' with our status to speak out?" he asked in 1971.[19] The following year, he exhorted students to "devote greater attention to planning the foundations of an Islamic state and studying the problems involved."[20]

If religion is the basis of legitimacy, what specifically within religion would make government legitimate? Ironically, it is not simply imposition of shari'a, Islamic law. Too often in contemporary political discourse, shari'a is treated as a uniform whole. In reality, in the Islamic world, there is no codified, consensus agreement on shari'a; different sects in Islam, and schools within those sects, differ in their acceptance of source material on the sayings and examples of the Prophet Muhammad and his associates, and they often have differing interpretations as to those sources that they collectively do accept. But even if Islamic law differs from region to region, do its local interpretations determine legitimacy? Here, too, the answer is not definitive.

Beginning in the 19th century, Middle Eastern states—whether independent, autonomous, or under colonial tutelage—created centralized, secular legal systems, usually borrowing from European models.[21] There was clerical resistance to such things in Iran, the Ottoman Empire, and Yemen, but, generally speaking, the substitution of Islamic law for European systems occurred without much resistance. Egypt became a model and Egyptian consultants common; personal status laws remained the domain of religious courts, while civil courts handled civil and criminal matters.

That there was not significant backlash is curious. George Washington University political scientist Nathan Brown argues that there was not more backlash because governments did not eliminate religious institutions such as courts, but rather augmented them with counterparts. But elsewhere, there was a long tradition of differentiation between religious and government institutions. In Mali, for example, there has been a half-millennium-old tradition of differentiation between religion and state, which contributed to the ease with which Mali embraced multiparty elections in 1992.[22]

Many Islamists today seek to strip away the foreign influence that they see in their government, culture, and society. Many of the most extreme—for example, those embracing al Qaeda or the Islamic State—believe that Islamic law dominated during Islam's Golden Age. This, however, is an exaggeration.[23] There was greater interplay among religions during the early period of Islam, and, indeed, interaction with Christians, Jews, and Zoroastrians left indelible marks on Islam and Islamic practice.[24]

Some unabashed proponents of an Islamic state did recognize this. Whereas many Islamists promise to impose shari'a—a slogan of the Muslim Brotherhood, for example, is "The Quran is our constitution"—Khomeini instead sought to create a separate constitution. He implied that neither an Islamic state nor religious legitimacy required exclusive application of Islamic law. In a 1988 letter to Ali Khamenei, Iran's president and, 18 months later, its supreme leader, Khomeini argued that the Islamic government did not have to "act within the framework of God's rules." He declared the Islamic Republic, as derivative of the Prophet's teachings, to be a primary rule of Islam and above the secondary rules such as fasting or the hajj.[25] In post-Saddam Iraq, the diversity of Islamic practice—not only between sects but between schools within each sect—led to a compromise in which Islam would be *a* source (rather than *the* source) for legislation with the caveat that no law could be passed that would not be in conformity with Islam.[26] Many other states followed suit: Even when leaders derive legitimacy in part from Islam, few states—Saudi Arabia and Sudan being the notable exceptions—deny space for adherents from other mainstream schools or practices.

Islam is certainly important. Should any government try to remove mention of Islam from its constitution, there would be rioting in the street and government collapse. But some countries have been exceptions: Mustafa Kemal Atatürk abolished the caliphate as he sought to raise Turkey from the ashes of the Ottoman Empire. When protests and even rebellions occurred, he crushed them with brute force. But even then, he did not fully separate religion and governance to the extent many believe. Turkey always tolerated religious organization and did not seek to completely exclude Islamist forces in the manner that secular socialist states such as Algeria, Saddam's Iraq, and Syria did. Turkey sponsors the Directorate of Religious Affairs (*Diyanet İşleri Başkanlığı*), which, as its name implies, regulates religious affairs. During the Kemalist era, the Diyanet sought to restrain more extremist interpretation, but under President Recep Tayyip Erdoğan, it has become an engine to further Islamism.

While Turkey, therefore, long retained the image of a country that promoted a separation of mosque and state, the question of religion's role in government was far less settled even in Kemalist times than many policymakers long believed.[27] In the last decades of the 20th century, it might have been possible to argue that Atatürk's revolution in Turkey proved the diminished importance of religion in establishing legitimacy. But religion's rebound under Erdoğan suggests that Atatürk's claims to legitimacy were far shallower than his followers cared to admit and that, quite simply, the ability to shroud leaders in Islam matters.

Lebanon perhaps presents the most interesting case study on the interplay between religion and sovereignty. The Lebanese constitution is confessional: It allocates positions based on religion, which, itself, is acknowledgment of the value of religious identity relative to nationalism for many, if not most, in Lebanon. Many Lebanese may complain about the confessional system, especially as the demographic realities of various communities change with time, but few would accept abandoning it for fear of suffering under the tyranny of the majority. While that might be a debate about governance, it is also one about legitimacy. Simply put, Christians and Sunnis would view a Shi'ite-dominated government as somehow less legitimate to their interests than one in which their own religious views are represented. Likewise, Muslims would find a Christian dictatorship illegitimate.

Nor is this notion of religious representation limited to Lebanon. One of the driving factors of Sunni opposition to the Assad regime in Syria is the sense that a state run by an Alawi minority is less legitimate than one that fully recognizes the Sunni majority in proportion to their population.

Are Monarchies the Key to Stability?

But if religion contributes to legitimacy, is religion alone enough? After all, protests have rocked the Islamic Republic of Iran repeatedly, and the backlash to the clerical establishment has also led to a rediscovery of Zoroastrianism and a spike in conversions to Christianity. Mohamed Morsi, a Muslim Brotherhood acolyte, won a tightly contested presidential election in 2012 but hemorrhaged public support in the run-up to the 2013 coup. In post–Arab Spring Tunisia, Islamists quickly lost power, and, in Iraq, the public has punished religious parties at the polls when they fail to deliver.

Indeed, the Arab Spring showed that governments can lose legitimacy when public frustration at their ineffectiveness boils over. The Arab Spring shocked the Middle East. While coups and revolutions were frequent across the Middle East and North Africa in the 1950s and 1960s, subsequent decades saw an ossification of leadership. When protestors ousted Ben Ali, it fractured the myth of inviolability. If Tunisians could rid their country of a leader who seemed determined to rule for life, so could Egyptians, Libyans, and Yemenis. As for Syrians, they might have as well, had it not been for foreign intervention to prop up Assad.

Simply put, dictators who had long assumed themselves to have popular legitimacy learned in an instant they had none. Decades of corruption, cronyism, and resentment of brutality came at a price. But, as republican counterparts were swept aside, regional monarchies remained standing.

That Arab monarchies were more stable than Arab republics has become conventional wisdom in many quarters. In countries that may be ethnically or tribally diverse, monarchs become unifying symbols. In Morocco, the king not only heads the state but also serves as *Amir al-Mu'minin*, commander of the faithful, and so claims religious legitimacy as well. So too does the king of Jordan, whose great-grandfather claimed to be the 38th-generation descendant from the Prophet Muhammad to cement a claim to legitimacy to lead a country that had no historical precedent. Saudi Arabia's kings use their role as "custodian of the two Holy Mosques" in Mecca and Medina to infuse their kingship with religious legitimacy.

But is there truth to the conventional wisdom? Perhaps not. In the 1950s, 1960s, and 1970s, coups and ideological revolutions swept aside monarchies in Egypt, Iran, Iraq, Libya, Syria, and Yemen. There was no magic formula to determine which monarchies survived and which fell. Syria's and Iraq's monarchies were recent colonial constructs, but so too was Jordan's surviving monarchy. Iran's history of kingship was thousands of years old when Muhammad Reza Shah fell. Yemen's and Libya's monarchs were swept aside despite the religious roles infused into the institution, and yet Morocco's kings continue to rule decades later. More recently, it is doubtful Bahrain's monarchy would have survived the Arab Spring had it not been for the intervention of Saudi Arabia.

F. Gregory Gause III, today the head of the International Affairs
Department at the Bush School of Government and Public Service at
Texas A&M University, has argued that monarchies are not especially
imbued with special cultural legitimacy. Rather, he suggests, Arab monarchies have used their wealth to co-opt opponents and, in the case of Jordan
and Morocco, while not particularly wealthy themselves, have benefited from
the largesse of oil-rich monarchies willing to help subsidize them.[28] While
Gause is right that oil wealth and the ability to use it to co-opt opposition
contributes to monarchies' stability, he may be underestimating other factors that contribute to the remaining monarchies' longevity.

Daniel Brumberg, a political scientist at Georgetown University, is
correct to observe that Arab monarchies have had an advantage because
they can wield power at a symbolic distance from the political arena and
can insulate themselves from the mendacity of daily politics.[29] Hence,
as protests in northern Morocco's impoverished Rif region accelerated
through 2017, both politicians and protestors sought the king's intervention and, by doing so, demonstrated the king's continued legitimacy.

Proponents of monarchy in the Middle East often argue that such
a system is inherently legitimate because monarchy is consistent with
Islamic norms. The 14th-century Tunisian historian Ibn Khaldun defined
four categories of just war in Islam, one of which was "dynastic against
secessionists and those who refuse obedience."[30] Indeed, while many
Islamic societies from their earliest years encouraged consultation,
modern revisionist writing about Islam being inherently democratic is
nonsense.[31] While the Prophet Muhammad's companions and immediate
successors were not hereditary rulers, within just a few decades both the
Shi'ites and then the Umayyad and Abbasid caliphates would set a precedent of hereditary rule.

Gause downplays the historic precedent argument by noting that
traditional hereditary leadership is merely a political construction that
strives to convince both subjects and outsiders of its legitimacy. While
he is correct that monarchies do not say they are based on popular will,
he still may be dismissing too readily the reach of history in shaping concepts of legitimacy.[32]

Do Social Contracts and Good Governance
Form the Basis of Legitimacy?

Simply put, it is wrong to transpose a Western notion of legitimacy onto the Middle East. In Western thought, there is a long literature about the nature of political societies. The fourth-century BC Greek philosopher Aristotle described political societies in which man ruled over other men as natural associations and spoke of the unequal power dynamics within families as a metaphor for a ruler over his subjects.[33] The 17th-century English philosopher Thomas Hobbes suggested a natural contract existed in which humans surrendered freedom to an absolute ruler in exchange for security. And compatriot John Locke believed that people subordinated their freedom to government to protect property and life. The 18th-century German philosopher Immanuel Kant argued that autonomy and authority were not mutually exclusive but that justice and civil society were only possible when humans entered into a community. For Hobbes, Locke, and 18th-century Genevan philosopher and writer Jean-Jacques Rousseau, power gained through consent was crucial to legitimacy.

The notion of a social contract between the ruler and ruled, however, is a relatively recent concept in the Islamic world and only truly entered the discourse during the late 19th century, especially regarding the idea of a "popular election."[34] Muhammad Rashid Rida, a late-19th- and early-20th-century Islamic reformer, argued that the Islamic community's sovereignty was manifested in the elite, the so-called "people of loosing and binding" (*ahl al-hall wa al-'aqd*), who were of a status that they could legitimately choose or depose a caliph.[35] In effect, this blessed oligarchy.

Whether or not dictatorship, oligarchy, or democracy prevailed, former Jordanian Foreign Minister Marwan Muasher, writing with Perry Cammack, a fellow in the Middle East Program at the Carnegie Endowment for International Peace, argued in their analysis of the Arab Spring that the absence or failures of social contracts were key to understanding the unrest. They wrote:

> Five years after the Arab Spring, the crisis of legitimacy that helped precipitate it has lost neither its resonance nor its urgency. . . . The objects of their [Arab] ire take many forms,

from authoritarianism and militarism to corruption and cronyism to external interference. These varied sources of discontent
highlight the underlying absence of meaningful social contracts
between states and citizens in most Middle Eastern countries.[36]

That may be true, but it still does not explain why so many Arab
states persist seemingly with legitimacy even as they lack meaningful
social contracts.

Quality of government certainly comes into play. Governance, as
Center for American Progress fellow Brian Katulis writes in this collection, varies widely in both type and quality. Some Middle Eastern countries
are monarchies, some are republics, and few are democracies. Some have
strong governments, while in others, such as Iraq and Lebanon, government is weak and power is diffuse. Nothing is necessarily wrong or surprising about this. After all, the Middle East is incredibly diverse, and one
size need not fit all.

Democracy might be a more ideal form of government than dictatorship, but that does not mean that all dictatorships are illegitimate. Some
Singaporeans complain about the social restrictions and lack of political
freedom in their city-state, but few deny the legitimacy of their government. The Quranic verse 4:59, "Obey God, obey His Prophet and obey
those in authority over you," can legitimize autocracy.[37] Egyptians, Syrians,
Tunisians, and Yemenis suffered the same repression but rose up in the
Arab Spring. Could the key to whether a government retains legitimacy or
loses it be not its form of government but rather its quality and its willingness to provide for its citizens?

Not necessarily. Both Islamic jurisprudence and tradition are
contradictory on the issue. The 10th-century Persian philosopher
Abu Nasr Muhammad ibn Muhammad al Farabi (known in the West
as Alpharabius) argued that rulers could not wage war simply to preserve their rule in the face of popular rebellion. Later, in both the
Ottoman period and early Turkish republic, citizens could petition the
sultan or the political leader to register complaints and seek redress.[38]
"The very existence of the regime was legitimized, at least in theory,
by attentiveness to the people's interest and welfare," Yiğit Akıt, an
assistant professor of history at Tulane University, wrote.[39]

However, while governments providing for their citizens may be the bedrock of a Western liberal notion of legitimacy, assuming that belief is universal would be a false assumption. While Iraqis complained about the lack of government services in the wake of the US-led invasion and Saddam Hussein's fall, when push came to shove, Shi'ites tended to rally around those parties that flew Shi'ite flags or embraced sectarian symbolism over those that actually delivered electricity, security, or clean water. The same held true for Iraqi Kurdish parties that have used nationalist rhetoric and symbolism to substitute for good governance. None of this should surprise.

There is long Islamic jurisprudence that prioritizes a citizen's loyalty to leadership over its quality to maintain loyalty. Badr al-Din Muhammad ibn Jama'a, a late-13th- and early-14th-century Syrian jurist, wrote:

> At a time when there is no imam and an unqualified person seeks the imamate and compels the people by his power and his armies, without any *bay'a* [oath of allegiance] or succession, then his *bay'a* is validly contracted and obedience to him is obligatory, so as to maintain the unity of the Muslims and preserve agreement among them.[40]

David Copp argued that morality of action should not necessarily be a factor to determine legitimacy because "*every* state owes its existence to some combination of events that includes a share of skullduggery, or worse."[41]

Nor does freedom necessarily matter. In 2001, Freedom House characterized Mali as the only free Muslim-majority country. By 2006, Senegal and Indonesia had joined Mali. But more than half of Muslim-majority countries were not free. Before the Arab Spring, there were no free Arab countries, and, today, Freedom House ranks only Tunisia as free. In contrast, in 2001 in the non-Muslim world, the majority of countries are free, with freedom expanding almost every year.[42]

Is There a Magic Formula to Legitimacy?

Social scientists and policymakers often seek to explain politics with magic, one-size-fits-all formulas or theories. They want US aid and assistance to bolster pro-American governments and solidify democracies. Nor would many shed tears if reactionary and revisionist states collapsed for lack of popular legitimacy, at least so long as they did not descend into chaos in the manner of post–Arab Spring Libya or Syria.

US administrations, regardless of political party, have embraced color revolutions across the globe. The Reagan administration embraced the 1986 People Power Revolution in the Philippines, which, in three days, ended the two-decade-long rule of dictator Ferdinand Marcos. President George H. W. Bush celebrated the fall of communist dictatorship in Eastern Europe, even if his enthusiasm, at least initially, did not extend to former Soviet republics such as Ukraine. George W. Bush embraced Pollyannaish thinking in the possibilities of a post-Saddam Iraq, believing that democracy would shape the legitimacy of any post-Saddam government. Obama likewise celebrated the Arab Spring, even if his enthusiasm wavered as civil war and violence erupted in the vacuums it created.

But is there a single variable or magic formula that imbues governments and states with legitimacy? No. States with age-old identities can have legitimacy, but so too can the most artificial constructs of the colonial era: Jordan, Qatar, and the United Arab Emirates. Religion can contribute to legitimacy, but seldom will it alone suffice. Indeed, it is a risky strategy. As the Iranian leadership has discovered, poor governance and corruption can easily soil the perceived legitimacy of religious clergy. Nor does any system of government insulate from popular uprisings when a magic formula develops.

Perhaps each state has its own formula. "The Saudi regime's legitimacy has been based upon a mix of religion, rentierism, patrimonialism, and tribalism,"[43] Arab world specialists Neil Quilliam and Maggie Kamel wrote. When Saudi authorities chose the wrong mix, it led to a collapse of the first Saudi state in 1818 and its second iteration in 1891.

While vast oil wealth might conceal broader problems with Saudi legitimacy, Saudi authorities recognize the necessity of reform. In March 1992, for example, King Fahd issued three new laws: Basic Law of Government, the Consultative Council Law, and the Law of Provinces. Each was meant to upgrade and formalize systems making Saudi Arabia, at least in theory, a more modern nation-state. In many ways, Crown Prince Muhammad bin Salman's Saudi 2030 reform plan continues to fit the pattern as the Saudi leadership seeks to pivot and reform to maintain its own legitimacy of rule.

In effect, reforms recognize that legitimacy is not a static concept and that states and governments need to pivot and evolve to maintain it.[44] A similar process exists in Jordan, where, Naval Postgraduate School Professor Glenn Robinson observed, the monarchy engages in preemptive reform "to maintain elite privilege in Jordan while limiting the appeal of more fundamental political change."[45]

Other strategies also augment state legitimacy. As its wealth grew, Saudi Arabia perfected a strategy by which it exported abroad and subsidized those too religiously radical for the kingdom, thereby ridding itself of an impending problem, at least in the short term.[46] Many other countries followed suit: For decades after the 1982 crackdown in Hama, the Assad family turned a blind eye and even supported Sunni radicals, so long as radical Islamists focused their attentions outside Syria. Many Gulf states likewise exported their own radicals so as to insulate themselves from challenges at home.

Sometimes, preserving legitimacy simply involves doing nothing to undermine it. A history of foreign interference has only added fuel to the conspiracy theories already permeating the Middle East. Foreign support for a regime or political figure can quickly delegitimize it or him.[47] This is one of the main themes with which Khomeini sought to delegitimize the shah, and Shi'ite firebrand Muqtada al-Sadr continues to use it to challenge those most closely associated with the United States and its military forces.[48]

There may be no magic formula to legitimacy, but the late Harvard University political theorist Samuel Huntington may have been onto something when he speculated that per capita income of $1,000–$3,000 in 1976 dollars was the threshold for democratization to begin.[49] If converted into 2017 dollars, then most Middle Eastern and North African countries exceed the threshold of $4,400–$13,200; only the Palestinian territories, Syria, and Yemen fall short. This means that states must increasingly pivot and evolve to retain legitimacy and stability.

Democratization is a long process, and, in a region where many citizens still embrace illiberal or collective values over individual liberty, it may not come soon. But the changes inherent in more affluent and educated societies, when coupled with new social media platforms for mobilization, could produce new and unpredictable challenges to government legitimacy. Perhaps what becomes most important, then, to retaining legitimacy is not nationalism, religion, or style of government, but rather the agility of any government to keep up with accelerating changes permeating societies.

Notes

1. Sandy Grady, "Go Ahead, Make My Departure! The Reagan-Gadhafi Show's Big Finish," *Miami Herald*, January 6, 1989; and James McCartney, "Sending a Message to Terrorists," *Miami Herald*, February 16, 1989.
2. G. Hossein Razi, "Legitimacy, Religion, and Nationalism in the Middle East," *American Political Science Review* 84, no. 1 (March 1990): 69.
3. David Hume, *A Treatise of Human Nature*, ed. L. Selby-Bigge (Oxford: Clarendon Press, 1978), 539.
4. David Copp, "The Idea of a Legitimate State," *Philosophy & Public Affairs* 28, no. 1 (Winter 1999): 10.
5. Copp, "The Idea of a Legitimate State," 26, 31.
6. Razi, "Legitimacy, Religion, and Nationalism in the Middle East," 70.
7. Magnus Bernhardsson, *Reclaiming a Plundered Past: Archaeology and Nationalism in Modern Iraq* (Austin, TX: University of Texas Press, 2005).
8. Geoffrey Bibby, *Looking for Dilmun* (New York: Knopf, 1969).
9. Quran 49:13.
10. Razi, "Legitimacy, Religion, and Nationalism in the Middle East," 78.
11. Razi, "Legitimacy, Religion, and Nationalism in the Middle East," 77.
12. Bernard Lewis, "Islamic Political Movements," *Middle East Review* 17 (1985): 23–27.
13. Razi, "Legitimacy, Religion, and Nationalism in the Middle East," 76.
14. See, for example, US Department of Homeland Security, "Remarks by Secretary of Homeland Security Jeh Johnson at the Islamic Society of North America's 53rd Annual Convention, 'The Promise and Wonder of This Country,'" September 3, 2016, https://www.dhs.gov/news/2016/09/03/remarks-secretary-homeland-security-jeh-johnson-islamic-society-north-america-s-53rd.
15. Shahrough Akhavi, "Sunni Modernist Theories of Social Contract in Contemporary Egypt," *International Journal of Middle East Studies* 35 (2003): 30.
16. Muhammad H. Naini, *Tanbih al-ommat va tanzih al-mellat ya hokumat az nazar-e Islam* [Exposition to the Nation and Refinement of the Believers, or Government from the Islamic Perspective] (Tehran: Enteshar, 1979).
17. Extract from *Kashf al-Asrar (Revelation of Secrets)*. Translation in Imam Khomeini, *Islam and Revolution*, trans. Hamid Algar (London: Kegan Paul, 1981), 170.
18. Ruhollah Khomeini, *Hukumat-i Islami* (Najaf: Nahzat-i Islami, 1391 [1971]). For an English translation, see Imam Khomeini, *Islam and Revolution*, trans. Hamid Algar (London: Kegan Paul, 1981), 27–166.
19. Imam Khomeini, "The Incompatibility of Monarchy with Islam," in *Islam and Revolution*, trans. Hamid Algar (London: Kegan Paul, 1981), 204.
20. Imam Khomeini, "Message to the Muslim Students in North America," in *Islam and Revolution*, trans. Hamid Algar (London: Kegan Paul, 1981), 210–11.
21. Nathan J. Brown, "Sharia and State in the Modern Middle East," *International Journal of Middle East Studies* 29, no. 3 (August 1997): 360.
22. Daniel Philpott, "Explaining the Political Ambivalence of Religion," *American Political Science Review* 101, no. 3 (August 2007): 516.

23. Hamid Enayat, *Modern Islamic Political Thought* (Austin, TX: University of Texas Press, 1982), 1.

24. Leor Halevi, *Muhammad's Grave: Death Rites and the Making of Islamic Society* (New York: Columbia University Press, 2011).

25. Razi, "Legitimacy, Religion, and Nationalism in the Middle East," 79; and Ruhollah Khomeini, "Ezhar-e Nazar-e Sarih va Mohemm-e maqam-e moazzam-e rahbari dar bareh-e ektiyarat-e motlaqeh-e hokumat-e eslami" [The clear and important expression of the leader's view on the absolute powers of the Islamic Government], *Ettela'at*, January 7, 1988.

26. Ashley S. Deeks and Matthew D. Burton, "Iraq's Constitution: A Drafting History," *Cornell International Law Journal* 40, no. 1 (Winter 2007): 8–9.

27. Umut Uzer, *An Intellectual History of Turkish Nationalism: Between Turkish Ethnicity and Islamic Identity* (Salt Lake City, UT: University of Utah Press, 2016).

28. F. Gregory Gause, "Kings for All Seasons: How the Middle East's Monarchies Survived the Arab Spring," Brookings Institution, September 24, 2013, 1, https://www.brookings.edu/research/kings-for-all-seasons-how-the-middle-easts-monarchies-survived-the-arab-spring/.

29. Daniel Brumberg, "Sustaining Mechanics of Arab Autocracies," *Foreign Policy*, December 19, 2011.

30. Lucian M. Ashworth, "Ibn Khaldun and the Origins of State Politics," in *Postcolonialism and Political Theory*, ed. Nalini Persram (Lanham, MD: Lexington Books, 2007), 46.

31. See, for example, Ahmed Subhy Mansour, "The Roots of Democracy in Islam," National Endowment for Democracy, December 16, 2002, http://www.ahl-alquran.com/English/show_article.php?main_id=4145.

32. Gause, "Kings for All Seasons," 9.

33. Donna Robinson Divine, "Legitimacy in Israel: How Important Is the State?," *International Journal of Middle East Studies* 10, no. 2 (May 1979): 207.

34. Akhavi, "Sunni Modernist Theories of Social Contract in Contemporary Egypt," 23.

35. Akhavi, "Sunni Modernist Theories of Social Contract in Contemporary Egypt," 29.

36. Perry Cammack and Marwan Muasher, "Arab Voices on the Challenges of the New Middle East," Carnegie Endowment for International Peace, February 12, 2016, 1, https://carnegieendowment.org/files/ArabExperts_Survey_English_final.pdf.

37. Bernard Lewis, "On the Quietist and Activist Traditions in Islamic Political Writing," *Bulletin of the School of Oriental and African Studies* 49, no. 1 (February 1986): 141.

38. Yiğit Akıtn, "Reconsidering State, Party, and Society in Early Republican Turkey: Politics of Petitioning," *International Journal of Middle East Studies* 39, no. 3 (2007): 437–38.

39. Akıtn, "Reconsidering State, Party, and Society in Early Republican Turkey," 442–43.

40. Lewis, "On the Quietist and Activist Traditions in Islamic Political Writing," 143.

41. Copp, "The Idea of a Legitimate State," 4.

42. Freedom House reports across multiple years are accessible at Freedom House, "About Freedom in the World," https://freedomhouse.org/report-types/freedom-world.

43. Neil Quilliam and Maggie Kamel, "Modernising Legitimacy: Saudi Strategies," *Alternatives: Turkish Journal of International Relations* 2, no. 2 (Summer 2003): 30, http://alternatives.yalova.edu.tr/article/view/5000159513.

44. Quilliam and Kamel, "Modernising Legitimacy," 44.

45. Glenn E. Robinson, "Defensive Democratization in Jordan," *International Journal of Middle East Studies* 30, no. 3 (August 1998): 387.

46. Quilliam and Kamel, "Modernising Legitimacy," 34.

47. Colin J. Beck, "Building as a Source of Islamic Political Organization," *Sociological Forum* 24, no. 2 (June 2009): 339.

48. Olivier Roy, "The Predicament of 'Civil Society' in Central Asia and the 'Greater Middle East,'" *International Affairs* 81, no. 5 (October 2005): 1010.

49. Samuel P. Huntington, *The Third Wave: Democratization in the Late Twentieth Century* (Norman, OK: University of Oklahoma Press, 1991), 63.

2

What Is the Role of Islam and Islamists in the Middle East?

A. KADIR YILDIRIM

Most contemporary analyses of the religion-politics relationship in the Middle East focus on Islam's distinctiveness. Islam, certain scholars charge, has always been unique in its relationship with politics. They say Islam is intrinsically a political religion and deem Islam particularly inimical to reform and modernization. Its presumed inability to adapt to contemporary secularism and, in modern times, its resistance to the privatization of religion—the process by which religion plays no major role in public life or policymaking and is largely constrained to the believer's private life—are merely symptoms of the essential qualities of Islam, the argument goes. Brookings Institution scholar Shadi Hamid called this "Islamic exceptionalism."[1]

However, such perspectives are not accurate for three reasons. First, they suggest that at a doctrinal level Islam sees no separation between the political and religious spheres. Second, they assume Islamic tradition has remained faithful to its doctrinal underpinnings throughout its long history. Third, they claim that Islamic tradition continued through modernity undisturbed by the changing political, economic, and social milieu of the societies in which it existed.

The intimate relationship between religion and state among Muslims in the premodern era was not unique; rather, it was the norm among religions at the time. The infusion between the political and religious spheres and the prominence of religious laws were key features. While Islam's initial encounter with modernity and secularism mirrored other religions' experiences, it differed both in the changing nature of its religious authority and the low level of religious institutionalization.

Islam was also unique for how these factors interacted with social, political, and economic conditions in the modern period to yield both discomfort with secularism and the contradictory conception in the Muslim mind that politics and religion are inseparable. This reaction to modernity and secularism has led contemporary Middle Eastern societies to regress on issues such as minority rights, pluralism, and core human values.

As the late Harvard scholar Shahab Ahmed documents, premodern Islam was marked by its high levels of heterogeneity and diversity.[2] It was not Islam's doctrinal principles that rendered it incapable of handling the challenge of the modern period, but rather the rise of a new crop of religious entrepreneurs—Islamists and Salafists—who took it upon themselves to counter modernity, secularism, and Western influence. In doing so, they embraced a revivalist and regressive approach to religion, essentially re-creating what they viewed as "authenticity" in Islamic beliefs and practice.

Religion-Politics Framework

Religion constitutes one of the most important dynamics of life across Middle Eastern societies. According to a recent Pew Research Center study, approximately 70 percent of Muslims in the region say religion is "very important" in their lives. In comparison, in Western societies, similar figures on the importance of religion stand at less than one-third of that of Middle Eastern societies.[3]

Conventional wisdom among both policymakers and the general public suggests that religion drives political developments, underlies violence, and instigates regional instability in the Middle East. Likewise, many regard Islam as a political system that is infused with religious doctrine and law. These two perspectives envision a causal relationship: Islam, as the most dominant factor in the lives of people in the Middle East and an inherently political religion, prompts political behavior and attitudes.

A range of data shows that Muslims in the Middle East favor an infusion of religion and politics. Pew survey data indicate that approximately two-thirds prefer religious leaders to have a political role (Figure 1). The shares of the population that seek Islamic law as the official law of the country hover around 70–80 percent across the Middle East, South Asia,

Figure 1. Median Percentage of Muslims Who Believe Religious Leaders Should Have Political Influence

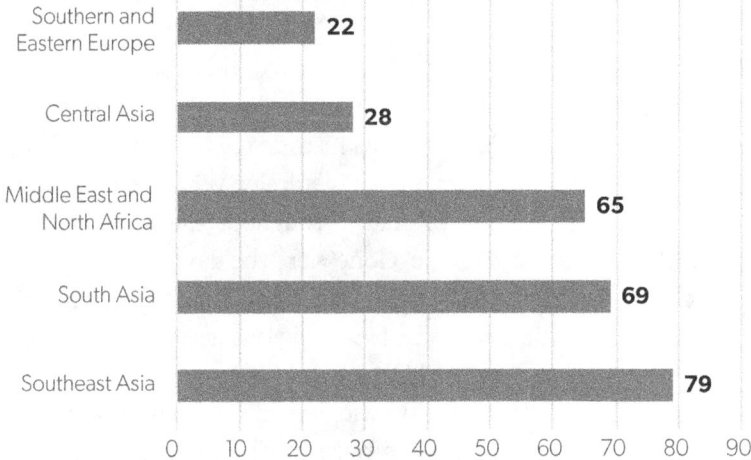

Region	Percentage
Southern and Eastern Europe	22
Central Asia	28
Middle East and North Africa	65
South Asia	69
Southeast Asia	79

0 10 20 30 40 50 60 70 80 90

Source: Pew Research Center, *The World's Muslims: Religion, Politics and Society,* April 20, 2013, https://www.pewforum.org/2013/04/30/the-worlds-muslims-religion-politics-society-overview/.

and Southeast Asia. But what motivates this demand for religion-politics infusion in the Middle East? And has the relationship between religion and politics always been this way?

The idea that political and religious realms are inseparable in Islam stems largely from the rising prominence of Islamism as a political ideology in the past century. Islamism has reshaped Islamic thinking on major political, social, and economic issues. Islamism, defined by Mohammed Ayoob—a prominent scholar of Middle Eastern religion and politics—as "a form of instrumentalization of Islam by individuals, groups and organizations that pursue political objectives" is a modern ideology that emerged at the turn of the 20th century on the heels of revivalist and puritan Salafi ideological thinking.[4] Islamists were deeply committed to the Islamic character of state and society and sought to correct practices they deemed "un-Islamic."[5]

The rise of political Islam and Salafism during this period was no coincidence. Politics of the day motivated Islamists to take action as they confronted issues such as colonialism and modernization and argued that Islam was the solution. If Islam could deliver answers to problems such as colonialism and backwardness, Islamists might argue, then the reason it had not worked in the past lay in the failures of those who wielded religious authority. Put differently, Islamists offered religious answers to political questions of the time.

What gave Islamists the opportunity to make their case and gain popularity was the void created after the gradual disappearance of the traditional clerical class (ulema). The ulema historically acted as the guardians of religion despite the lack of an official hierarchy. With the onset of modernization and centralization of state throughout the Middle East, the ulema saw their positions degrade. Gone were the days when anyone who claimed religious authority or wanted to speak on behalf of Islam was subject to the ulema's critical scrutiny. New religious actors such as the Islamists found an opportunity in which they not only could speak for Islam but also were accepted as legitimate wielders of religious authority. Their timing was impeccable. The masses were waking up to popular politics, and increasing levels of education and mass media consumption were preparing the masses for the messages of new political actors.

This was a momentous change in the religion-politics relationship in the Middle East. The significance was due to not only how it reshaped the field of religious actors but also how it affected religion's role in public life and public discussions on major issues. Consider two examples: homosexuality and Islamic law.

Historically, homosexuality has not been a major concern in the Middle East. It was neither publicly embraced nor encouraged, yet homosexuals largely found tolerance. Religiously, while homosexuality was regarded as a religious offense, homosexuals were comfortable even at the mosque, and Islamic jurisprudence collections addressed ways to accommodate homosexuals in society.[6]

Likewise, shari'a, Islamic law, had been the backbone of the legal infrastructure throughout the Middle East in the premodern period, although it was by no means the sole law of the land. Secular legislation existed in ample supply. With the rise of modern nation-states, states tried codifying and secularizing the legal structure. In fact, this move toward secular legislation was so well established that it was rarely questioned or challenged until the last decades of the 20th century. It was only with the fall from grace of secular nationalist ideologies that the popular perception of

Figure 2. Percentage of Muslims Who Favor Making Shari'a the Official Law in their Country

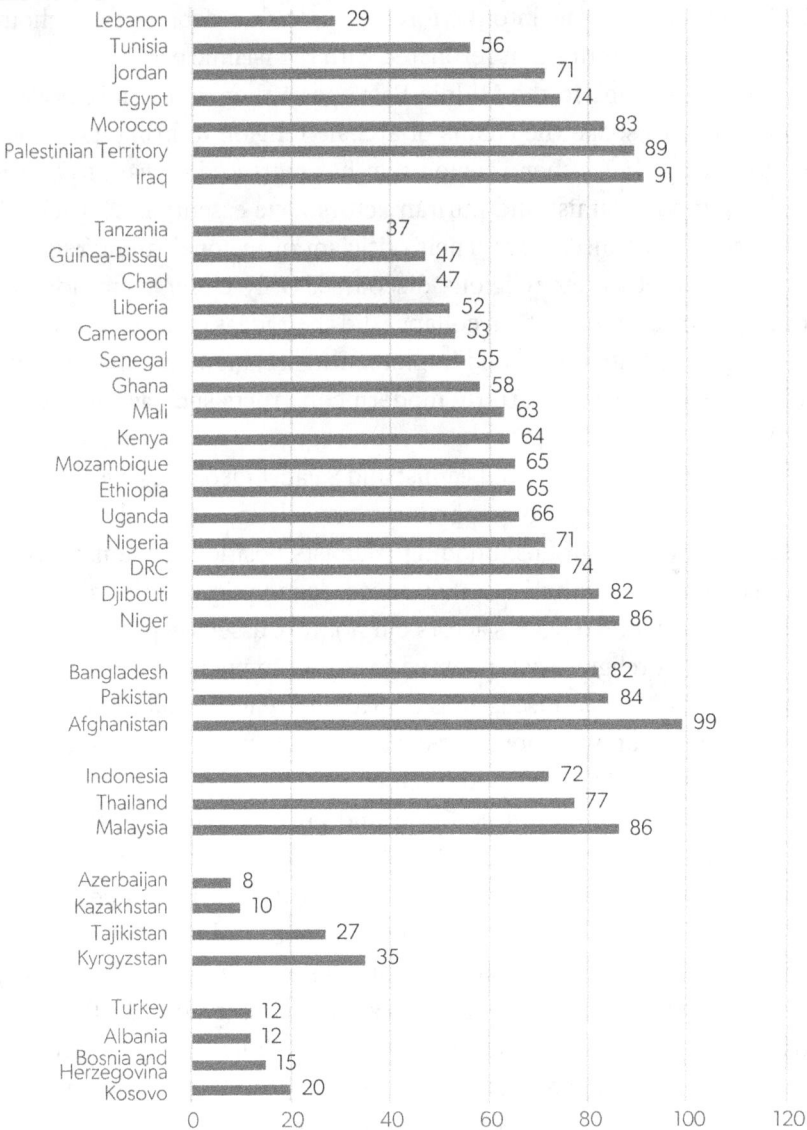

Country	Percentage
Lebanon	29
Tunisia	56
Jordan	71
Egypt	74
Morocco	83
Palestinian Territory	89
Iraq	91
Tanzania	37
Guinea-Bissau	47
Chad	47
Liberia	52
Cameroon	53
Senegal	55
Ghana	58
Mali	63
Kenya	64
Mozambique	65
Ethiopia	65
Uganda	66
Nigeria	71
DRC	74
Djibouti	82
Niger	86
Bangladesh	82
Pakistan	84
Afghanistan	99
Indonesia	72
Thailand	77
Malaysia	86
Azerbaijan	8
Kazakhstan	10
Tajikistan	27
Kyrgyzstan	35
Turkey	12
Albania	12
Bosnia and Herzegovina	15
Kosovo	20

Source: Pew Research Center, *The World's Muslims: Religion, Politics and Society,* April 20, 2013, https://www.pewforum.org/2013/04/30/the-worlds-muslims-religion-politics-society-overview/; and Pew Research Center, *Tolerance and Tension: Islam and Christianity in Sub-Saharan Africa,* April 15, 2010, https://www.pewforum.org/2010/04/15/executive-summary-islam-and-christianity-in-sub-saharan-africa/.

Islamic law began to change (Figure 2). The rise of Islamist groups in the post-1970s period and their criticisms of ruling secular regimes success-fully brought Islamic law into the forefront of public debates throughout the Middle East in terms that resonated with the Islamic past.[7]

What is occurring in the Middle East today, then, is not a backward region failing to shake the chains of archaic religion to bring itself into the modern age but rather a region that has regressed in ways to a pre-modern period. Islamist and puritan actors have essentially "hijacked" Islam and Islamic discourse.[8] Their criticism of regional ruling regimes lent legitimacy to their religious discourse. Only under conditions of economic, social, and political collapse did their ideas gain currency. The obsession with state power and implementing religious visions via state institutions gave birth to utterly modern constructs such as the idea of the "Islamic state."[9]

Such extensive influence of Islamist and Salafist ideologies over Islamic thinking does not always correspond to overwhelming electoral or popular support for Islamist groups. Budding Islamists positioned themselves as legitimate religious authorities; they succeeded in part because more tra-ditional or authentic religious actors did not take assertive public roles. If and when other religious actors opted to engage in public discussions and opine on certain issues, discussions turned into religious bidding contests to see which group was more conservative, authentic, and Islamic. Reli-gious competition drove religious politics.

Take, for example, post-2011 Egypt and public discussions about the new constitution and elections. The Muslim Brotherhood was the best-organized political group in the country. For the first time in decades, it had an opportunity to compete in elections freely, and it was open to col-laborating with other groups and was not interested in dominating. Reality did not match its rhetoric, however, as a more conservative Brotherhood took hold as the interim government moved to draft a new constitution. Why? The Nour Party and other hard-line Salafists popped up right after the revolution and garnered significant popular interest.

As Salafists demanding Islamic law began chipping away at the Broth-erhood's traditional support base, the Brotherhood embraced a similarly conservative political discourse to reclaim supporters peeled away by the Salafists. The Brotherhood dropped self-restraint and decided to run a candidate in the presidential election—and a greater number of candidates in parliamentary races than it had previously promised—and it pushed on with the constitution drafting despite the secular parties' protests.[10] This strategy contrasted sharply with the Tunisian Ennahdha party's policy of self-restraint in both government and the constitution-drafting process after the revolution, as well as its subsequent adoption of Muslim democracy as party ideology, formally dropping references to Islamist ideology in party program. The absence of religious competition from more conservative Islamist groups is one of the crucial factors to explain Ennahdha's evolution in recent years.

Islamic Reformation

Many Western politicians and policymakers place their hopes in reform in Islam and sometimes call openly for it. President Barack Obama's address to the Islamic world in 2009 is one such example of an attempt to trigger a discussion and such (implicit) calls for "reformation" in Islam.[11] Too often, however, such calls for reform are made without any sense of the current state of reformist debates.

The idea of reform in Islam is not new. The late 19th and early 20th centuries, in particular, witnessed the emergence of many reformist movements. They stood on solid religious ground. The Quran, Islam's primary reference and, according to believers, the word of God, urges believers to engage in reform (*islah*). A corresponding prophetic tradition envisions a religious reformer for each century, so the question of whether Islam is open to reform has little relevance. The real question is what lies beneath the inability to engage in a sustained reform effort in Islam and the Muslim world. The answer lies in the "politics of Islamic reform," to employ the terminology of Saba Mahmood, professor of anthropology at the University of California, Berkeley.[12]

Too often, reformism gets intertwined in the West with frustration over unfulfilled expectations. Part of the reason for this is that for many theologians and Muslims, reform is not synonymous with Western conceptions of the word. Reform, for example, does not necessarily mean progress. American pundits assume that reform is progressive and desirable and that reform will help Muslim societies reach modernization and become more pluralist and inclusive. But just as reform can be forward-looking and progressive, it can conversely be backward-facing and regressive.

Two distinct developments gave rise to the early calls for reform among Muslims in the early modern period. On one hand, European powers occupied various parts of the Middle East. The European expansion in the Middle East and the subsequent decline of the authority of Muslim rulers contradicted most Muslims' convictions about the divinely ordained order of things that were in place for many centuries. Moreover, Muslim rulers seemed unable to respond to the challenge Europeans posed. This was a major shock.

On the other hand, the slowly expanding gap between Europe and the Middle East in industrialization and material progress over the past few centuries finally led many in the region to submit that the Middle East was, indeed, left behind. It was not until their lives were directly affected by this gap that Muslims began thinking about the causes of their underdevelopment.

Muslims perceived these developments in dramatically different ways and reached different conclusions. One camp envisioned no fundamental problem with the existing structure of state, society, or religion. Rather, the core problems were with how Muslims carried themselves and with their moral degeneration. They believed that Muslims themselves needed to engage in "personal reform" in their lax ways of practicing their faith and return to the pristine Islam of the Golden Age, when the Prophet Muhammad and his companions lived. After the Golden Age, faith was fettered with innovations that polluted religion's purity, proponents of this argument claimed. Reform efforts were therefore geared toward revivalism, turning back the clock in the Muslim world.

Such early calls for personal reform and a return to Islamic Golden Age are primarily associated with Salafism (and its Saudi edition, Wahhabism). In some sense, the origins of this effort can be traced back to the writings of Ibn Taymiya and Ibn Qayyim al-Jawziyah, 13th- and 14th-century Islamic scholars. Nonetheless, the true rise of revivalism was set in motion when the puritan religious leader Muhammad Ibn Abd al-Wahhab struck an agreement with Muhammad bin Saud in 18th-century Arabia. This agreement tied the theocratic nature of the future Saudi state to its absolutist political character.

The scripturalist tendency of revivalist reform aimed to return Islam to the early tenets of the holy texts. Such revival and personal reform would combat not only the West's cultural transgressions and colonialism, revivalists argued, but also the West's secular and materialist mindset. Because Islamic revivalism concerns itself with political goals, it selectively draws from religious texts to justify its reforms. Revivalist reform efforts included figures such as Ahmad Brelwi in India (1786–1831), Hajji Shariatullah (1781–1840) and the Faraizi movement in Bengal, Emir Abdelkader (1808–83) in Algeria, and Muhammad Ahmad (1844–85) in the Sudan.

While some looked for inspiration in the past, other reformists embraced a more forward-looking reform agenda. They acknowledged that societal changes over the centuries required a new approach to religion. Muslim leaders who visited Europe, in particular, were more forceful in their calls for reform and often criticized the religious establishment. In particular, the ulema came under fire for being an obstacle to modernization and reform.

More specifically, critics charged the religious establishment with prioritizing its own corporate interests society's. Reformists charged the ulema with "traditionalism, obscurantism, and antiscientific tendencies," setting back progress in Muslim societies and standing as obstacles to other "reform agendas" in society as "bastions of obsolete orthodoxy in need of comprehensive reforms."[13] Some reformers in this group observed a "happy coincidence" between European-style reforms and what the core values of the religion and the sacred texts demanded. Individuals such as Sayyid Jamal ad-Din al-Afghani and Muhammad Abduh were at the forefront of such calls.[14]

Indeed, some early progress seemed to track this along the lines of this second group's vision. Secular governments that rose to power on the heels of independence movements pursued religious reform. These reforms mimicked progressive reform agendas that envisioned eliminating the influence of religious establishment, privatizing religion, and establishing secularism as a principle of government. Yet, despite the headway made in progressive reforms, a number of factors have not only stopped reforms but also pushed societies further back into regressivity.

Beginning with Atatürk's and Reza Shah's in the 1920s and 1930s in Turkey and Iran, respectively, secular governments throughout the region embarked on top-down reforms to curb, if not eliminate, the religious establishment's influence on public life. They found some success. However, from the 1970s onward, this changed as governments' inability to provide progress on social, economic, and political issues and to deliver on their modernization promises opened space for regressive reformers to question the entire basis of secular governance. Modest gains in social modernization were not accompanied by political modernization. Masses had few opportunities to voice their needs, concerns, and frustrations.

Political Islam revived as Islamists seized advantage of the policy failures of secular governments. Islamist actors infused religious discourse with political criticism to tap into the masses' social, economic, and political frustrations across the region. Religion was presented as the answer to their woes. Islamist discourse resonated well with the religiously inclined and marginalized masses.

Islamists' religious discourses remain a throwback to the early revivalist and rear-facing forms of Islamic reform. The path to progress, they argued, required a return to "authentic" Islam resting on Islamic norms, shari'a, and an Islamic state. Development and progress would be moral and in line with Islamic values and would avoid the decadence of Western societies.

In reality, the Islam proposed by Islamists and Salafists was not in full harmony with the Islam of the premodern period. Critically, Islamists envisioned an Islam that would be a degenerate form of premodern Islam. For example, shari'a has emerged as a contentious issue in recent decades. Unlike its contemporary conceptions, shari'a was understood to be a human effort to approximate the Divine Will and, therefore, an imperfect and inherently flawed process.[15]

Multiple schools of thought competed on what Islamic jurisprudence was, typically eschewing absolute legal statements. In this spirit, incremental changes, or "mini-reformations," took place over time that recognized changes in social context.[16] Making Islamic law was a private enterprise, largely autonomous from the state. By contrast, the type of shari'a that today's Islamists call for is marked by state control, absolutism, and a static nature.

It is also striking to note the regression from early forms of Islam regarding minority rights. Contemporary Muslim societies have fallen behind older societies in pluralism and inclusiveness on issues such as homosexuality and religious minority rights. Premodern books of Islamic jurisprudence included provisions on how to accommodate homosexuals in society and inside mosques. By contrast, homosexuals are presently ostracized from society, condemned to death in many countries in the name of Islam. Similarly, various ethnic and religious minorities face high levels of discrimination.

In this regard, an unmistakable correlation exists between the rise to prominence since the 1970s of Islamist and Salafist groups and their ideologies and the emergence of a puritanical Islam that calls for regressive and revivalist Islamic reformism.

Why and how do Islamists and Salafists command public religious discourse so effectively? Why do others, presumably legitimate religious authorities, not oppose these views that are determined to set back any recent efforts for more progressive reform in the Muslim world? The answers to these questions lie partly in the nature of religious authority in Islam.

While Shi'ism institutionalizes religious authority, a hierarchy exists, and the clergy's privileged position in faith is assured by the acceptance that Islamic scholars are heirs to the prophet's mission, religious authority is not centralized. Sunni Islam—today followed by perhaps 85–90 percent of Muslims—decentralized religious authority to a far greater degree. There is no consensus religious authority to credential religious authority. In Islam, and in Judaism, there are no formal initiations into the "priesthood" or religious leadership, as both Protestantism and Catholicism embrace. Islamic religious authority rests largely on individual choice to follow specific religious figures that a Muslim believes knowledgeable and worthy of respect. Respect is earned rather than conferred.[17]

Historically, the ulema have exerted quasi-control over Islamic religious authority through a pact between religious and political leaders in which political leaders would uphold Islamic law in return for the ulema's legitimation of the political authority.[18] This pact broke down at the turn of the 20th century as codification of shari'a and modernization of the legal system catalyzed the transformation of the religious authority and facilitated the rise of new religious actors.

Most Islamist and Salafist actors emerged in this period and gradually assumed greater visibility and voice in the public sphere. Because there is no centralized or hierarchical official religious authority within Sunni Islam to differentiate between the legitimacy of religious authorities, Islamist actors successfully co-opted popular religious sentiment in their quest for greater political and religious influence. Islamists have cast themselves as the proponents of conventional religious wisdom; followers accepted their puritan certitudes as mainstream Islamic doctrine at a time when the traditional religious authorities were in no position to challenge them. Major segments of the non-Islamist population also bought into Islamists' religious discourse even when they did not support Islamist parties.

In view of the Islamist and Salafist dominance streak in recent decades, the progressive Islamic reform efforts have largely been marginal, ineffective, and ultimately an elite affair, lacking the popular demand and support for such reforms. Syrians Muhammad Shahrur and Sadiq Jalal al-Azm, Moroccan Said bin Said, and Iranian Abdolkarim Soroush have each proposed reforms in recent decades. However, Islamists typically dismissed as heresy their arguments to reform religious establishment and to rethink Islamic texts in light of modern social, political, and economic conditions.

Moreover, the puritan approach to religion was so potent that it permeated virtually every corner of Muslim societies. For example, when Tunisia moved to become the first Arab state to establish equality in inheritance between men and women in 2017, Ahmed Al-Tayeb, the grand imam of Al-Azhar in Egypt, declared, "Al-Azhar rejects categorically the intervention of any policy or regulations that affect/change the beliefs of the Muslims or the rulings of their Sharia or tamper with them. . . . There is no room for re-interpretation, and it is not accepted by the public or non-specialists, whatever their culture."[9]

Considering the lack of popular demand for reform in Islam and charismatic leadership to drive such reform, expectations for a process analogous to the Protestant Reformation remain unfounded. Islamists have successfully tied their conservative Islamic rhetoric to the (il)legitimacy of existing governments. They claim that existing models of secular governance fail to deliver because they are insufficiently Islamic and that decades of secular governance have compounded problems throughout the region, such as unemployment, lack of development, inequality, and political suppression.

Unless and until the Islamist critique of secular governance can be decoupled from its religious component, imagining a sociopolitical context in which Islamic reform can be successfully debated is hard. Decades of Islamist and Salafist indoctrination have created an environment in which the competition for Islamic ideas occurs exclusively within the conservative end of the religious ideological spectrum. Religious actors, as political entrepreneurs, are aware of where the religious competition lies and up the ante with their discourse and dogma accordingly.

Improved governance and delivery of educational, economic, and health care outcomes remain essential to this process of decoupling. The perceived ineptitude of secular governments in delivering basic services has been a religiously charged grievance of Islamists for several decades. The priority in paving the way for any reform effort requires ensuring that basic policy outcomes can be delivered effectively to neuter criticisms through a religious prism. So long as Islamist cries against economic and political instability and inequality remain justified, little progress can be made in Islamic reform efforts.

Sectarianism

Another topic of interest in contemporary polemics surrounding Islam is the sectarian division between Sunnis and Shi'ites. At its origin, the division was primarily a political rift, rooted in the dispute over who would succeed the Prophet Muhammad as the Muslim community's political leader following his death in 632 AD. Before his death, Muhammad did not designate a successor or identify a mechanism to determine political leadership in his aftermath. As a result, two major positions emerged in the subsequent debate.

The first advocated for a merit- and piety-based leadership and believed those who were most qualified and had the ability to lead in the prophet's footsteps should assume leadership. The second called for lineage-based succession. The caliph, for this second group, must come from the prophet's family, specifically from the bloodline of Ali, the prophet's cousin and son-in-law.

Disagreements continued through the tenure of the first four caliphs and, on occasion, led to armed clashes. The eventual break came about when an assassin murdered Ali and the Umayyad family claimed the caliphate. Followers of Ali opposed the Umayyad family's legitimacy and authority. The partisans of Ali—the Shi'at Ali—became known as Shi'ites, while the majority who continued to recognize the Umayyad caliphate's legitimacy were called Sunnis, from the Arabic word for tradition, a reference to following the tradition—sunna—of the Prophet Muhammad.

While the origins of the separation between the two sects were political, it catalyzed religious separation as well. The two sects agreed on the Quran as God's verbatim word, but differences emerged in the authenticity of various recollection and records of the Prophet Muhammad's sayings and actions (hadith), which eventually led to "diverging traditions of ritual, law and practice."[20] The centrality of the prophet's bloodline ensured a more hierarchical clergy for Shi'ites. By contrast, the Sunnis lacked a comparable hierarchical structure of religious authority, embracing a free market of religious authority.

Despite the diverging religious traditions, the discord between the two rarely ventured into an outright religious conflict; historically, both sides generally shied away from disparaging the other sect's religious authenticity, although there were exceptions. For example, conservative Sunni religious scholar Ibn Taymiya (1263–1328), whose teaching subsequently inspired Wahhabism, denounced Shi'ites as "rejecters of faith."[21]

Nonetheless, such denunciations of Shi'ites by the Sunni fundamentalist fringe was long the exception rather than the rule. Indeed, in 1959, Sheikh Mahmoud Shaltut, who as rector of Al-Azhar University in Cairo was a preeminent Sunni authority, issued a ruling that officially recognized Shi'ism as a fifth school of Islamic jurisprudence, on equal footing with the four main Sunni schools.[22]

Political conflict between the two sects was more common, and, on occasion, this erupted into warfare, most notably in the 16th and 17th centuries, when Sunni Ottomans and the Shi'ite Safavids often fought. In the late 20th century, sectarian conflict again erupted in Lebanon and with the Iran-Iraq War, and, today, sectarian conflicts have spread to Bahrain, Syria, Yemen, and elsewhere. Such political sectarian conflicts are generally of three types: minorities suppressed by majority rule (e.g., Saudi Arabia), a majority suppressed by minority rule (e.g., Bahrain and Syria), or conflict between Sunni- and Shi'ite-ruled countries (e.g., Iran and Saudi Arabia).

Figure 3. Percentage of Muslims Who Say Sunni-Shi'ite Tension Is a Big Problem in Their Country

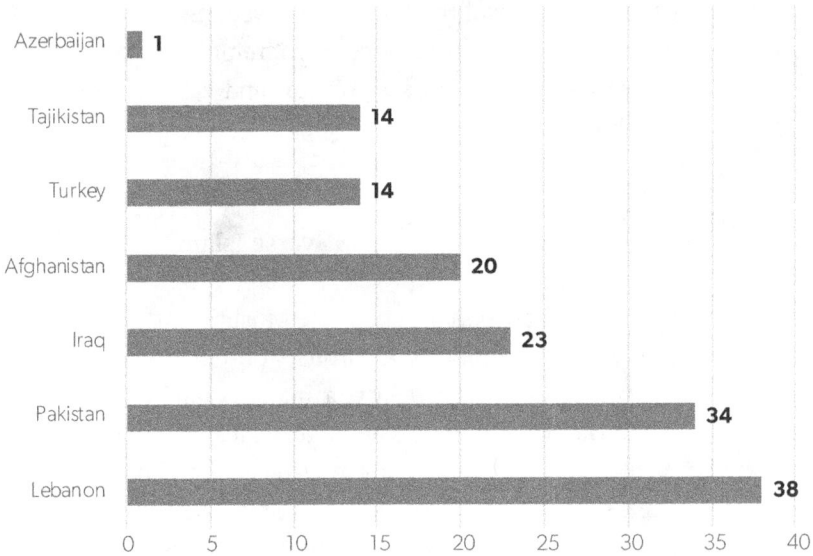

Azerbaijan	1
Tajikistan	14
Turkey	14
Afghanistan	20
Iraq	23
Pakistan	34
Lebanon	38

(x-axis: 0, 5, 10, 15, 20, 25, 30, 35, 40)

Source: Pew Research Center, *The World's Muslims: Religion, Politics and Society*, April 20, 2013, https://www.pewforum.org/2013/04/30/the-worlds-muslims-religion-politics-society-overview/.

Political alliances between Sunnis and Shi'ites are as frequent as the conflicts. For example, Shi'ite Iran supports the Sunni Hamas organization, and Saudi Arabia has recently courted Iraqi Shi'ite leader Muqtada al-Sadr. Turkey and Iran have recently drawn closer together, and Hezbollah enjoys support from some Lebanese Christian and Sunni factions. In each case, the conflict revolves less around converting or eradicating the other and more about establishing control over domestic or regional power.

In this regard, the Islamic State's anti-Shi'ite discourse was a further reflection of the political concern with Shi'ites' rising prominence in the region. As Melani Cammett, professor of politics at Harvard, observed, sectarian animosity is not the "root cause" of conflicts like the Syrian civil war, but "rather, the hyperpoliticization of sectarian identities is one of the outcomes—and an increasingly salient one as conflict progresses. The origins of the Syrian war lie in much more mundane political and economic grievances."[23]

A Pew survey found that only a small minority in various countries in the region views the Sunni-Shi'ite divide as "a very big problem" (Figure 3). At the popular level the tensions between Sunnis and Shi'ites are not perceived as a major source of concern, reinforcing the idea that the Sunni-Shi'ite tensions are largely political and reflect the ongoing geopolitical rivalries in the region.

Does Geography Make a Diverse Islam?

One of the common misconceptions about the Muslim world is that Arabs constitute the bulk of its inhabitants. A corollary observation is that Arabs represent the typical Muslim. In reality, a majority of Muslims world-wide lives outside the Middle East. The largest Muslim populations are all located in South and Southeast Asia: Bangladesh, India, Indonesia, and Pakistan. Muslims in the Middle East make up a smaller share of the global Muslims across the world (around 31 percent), and Arabs even a smaller fraction (around 21 percent).

There are two major differences between Islam as practiced in the Middle East and Islam in the rest of Asia. Islam arrived in South and Southeast Asia much later compared to its quick and early penetration into Middle Eastern and North African societies. Certain parts of Indonesia did not Islamize until the 18th century.[24]

In addition, when Islam arrived in South and Southeast Asia, it met and interacted with local mystical traditions, in addition to Hinduism and Buddhism.[25] The result was a sort of Islamic syncretism that incorporated many practices that would render these Muslims heterodox. The predominance of Sufi practices with major non-Islamic elements largely defined these heterodox Muslim groups. This process is similar to the syncretic Muslim experience among Sufi Muslims in West African countries such as Mali, Niger, and Senegal.

Developments in recent periods have eroded some of Islam's diversity. Three interrelated factors help explain these crucial developments. First, in the early 20th century, increasing interactions with the Middle East, in particular with revivalist and Islamist trends, pushed Muslims in South Asia, and to a lesser degree in Southeast Asia, to rethink their religious syncretism.[26] In particular, the interaction led to a greater codification of Islamic rules and a greater emphasis on the Quran and the hadith in Asian Muslim practice. Muslims in Asia began questioning their Muslim identity, what true religious practice should be, and how religion should shape their lives. Greater literacy and education catalyzed this process of "objectification."[27] Islamist actors' rise to prominence as part of the anti-colonial movements in the region intensified this process.

Second, Muslims from Asian regions increasingly integrated themselves into the transnational networks of Islamist groups. Especially important in this context is how South and Southeast Asian Muslims viewed Middle Eastern Islam and Salafism as the genuine representation of the Islamic model. Integration into transnational Islamist networks provided, for them, further legitimacy to the Islamic credentials of Asian Muslims as "faithful members of the *umma*."[28] The new generation of young Muslims was quite receptive to Islamist and Salafist ideas of how Islam can be a solution to their problems.

Lastly, the windfall profits in the aftermath of the 1970s oil shocks for Saudi Arabia prompted a fundamental shift in the trajectory of Islam and Islamic practice in Asia. Asia provided a unique opportunity for the Wahhabi evangelicals to preach their vision. Saudi clerics possessed both the "authentic" religious clout with their puritanism and the funds to flourish their ideological outlook on the eager who looked up to the Saudis as true representatives of Muslim faith and practice.

Recent studies shed light on how this perception of Wahhabi Islam as a source of genuine Islamic authority shapes the attitudes of Muslims in Asia. Quintan Wiktorowicz, an expert on Islamic movements, found that many Muslims use "cognitive shortcuts" to assess religious authority and credibility of various religious actors.[29] The fact that Islam does not have a centralized or hierarchical structure of religious authority facilitates recourse to cognitive shortcuts. This condition is particularly acute under conditions in which religious heterogeneity is high.

Wiktorowicz found that those Muslims who are less knowledgeable about Islam were more tractable to extremists' religious arguments and, ultimately, ideologies. Building on Wiktorowicz's insight, Georgetown University scholars Christine Fair, Jacob Goldstein, and Ali Hamza conducted a survey in Pakistan to test whether level of knowledge of

Islam affects Muslims' political attitudes. They found that higher levels of knowledge of Islam do, indeed, suppress support for terrorism and violence among Pakistani Muslims.[30]

These studies suggest that Asian Muslims who historically harbor a high level of Islamic heterogeneity display a disproportionate susceptibility to the authority, authenticity, and religious ardor that religious puritans such as Wahhabis and Salafists claim. This observation raises the specter that over the past several decades, financial and ideological influx of Wahhabi and Islamist thought and movements rendered the differences that once existed between the Muslims of the Middle East and Asia virtually nonexistent.

Implications

Religion is crucial to Middle East politics and will continue being so. In the past several decades, Islamists and Salafis have shaped the public role of religion throughout the region. Their impact not only is limited to shaping values and policies that relate to identity and cultural issue areas but also affects domestic and regional politics. This influence is amplified by the increasing number of Islamist parties that assume governmental roles and transnational actors that emerged as vital players in regional politics. While Islamist actors are not the sole source of instability, they do have a disproportionate effect on how Middle Eastern politics and societies evolve. What are the implications of such infusion of religion and politics for the future of regional politics?

So long as the Islamist, puritan outlook continues to dominate ideological and policy orientation of the region, the outlook for the Middle East with domestic policy, democratization, and regional political stability will be bleak. If more progressive reformists are to decouple religious discourse from public policy issues, governments must resolve these problems. Ultimately, the legitimacy of religious discourse as a viable public policy option rests on the failure of secular policies, not on the merits of religious discourse. Improving educational, health, and income outcomes can go a long way in paving the way for resolving Islam's challenge with the modern nation-state.

Notes

1. Shadi Hamid, *Islamic Exceptionalism: How the Struggle over Islam Is Reshaping the World* (New York: St. Martin's Press, 2016).

2. Shahab Ahmed, *What Is Islam? The Importance of Being Islamic* (Princeton, NJ: Princeton University Press, 2015).

3. Angelina E. Theodorou, "Americans Are in the Middle of the Pack Globally When It Comes to Importance of Religion," Pew Research Center, December 23, 2015, http://www.pewresearch.org/fact-tank/2015/12/23/americans-are-in-the-middle-of-the-pack-globally-when-it-comes-to-importance-of-religion/.

4. Mohammed Ayoob, *The Many Faces of Political Islam: Religion and Politics in the Muslim World* (Ann Arbor, MI: University of Michigan, 2008), 2.

5. Amit Bein, *Ottoman Ulema, Turkish Republic: Agents of Change and Guardians of Tradition* (Stanford, CA: Stanford University Press, 2011), 24; and Dale F. Eickelman and James P. Piscatori, *Muslim Politics* (Princeton, NJ: Princeton University Press, 1996), 44.

6. Stephen O. Murray and Will Roscoe, *Islamic Homosexualities: Culture, History, and Literature* (New York: New York University Press, 1997); and Samar Habib, "Queer-Friendly Islamic Hermeneutics," *ISIM Review* 21, no. 1 (Spring 2008): 32–33.

7. Noah Feldman, *The Fall and Rise of the Islamic State* (Princeton, NJ: Princeton University Press, 2008), 6.

8. Khaled Abou El Fadl, *The Great Theft: Wrestling Islam from the Extremists* (San Francisco, CA: HarperOne, 2007).

9. Wael Hallaq, *The Impossible State: Islam, Politics, and Modernity's Moral Predicament* (New York: Columbia University Press, 2012).

10. Nathan J. Brown, "Contention in Religion and State in Postrevolutionary Egypt," *Social Research: An International Quarterly* 79, no. 2 (Summer 2012): 531–50.

11. David A. Graham, "A Short History of U.S. Presidents Explaining Islam to Muslims," *Atlantic*, May 21, 2017, https://www.theatlantic.com/international/archive/2017/05/american-presidents-explain-islam-to-muslim/527415/.

12. Saba Mahmood, "Secularism, Hermeneutics, and Empire: The Politics of Islamic Reformation," *Public Culture* 18, no. 2 (2006): 323–47.

13. Bein, *Ottoman Ulema*, 24.

14. B. A. Roberson, *Shaping the Current Islamic Reformation* (New York: Routledge, 2003).

15. Khaled Abou El Fadl, *Speaking in God's Name: Islamic Law, Authority and Women* (Oxford, UK: Oneworld Publications, 2001).

16. Roberson, *Shaping the Current Islamic Reformation*.

17. Bryan S. Turner, "Religious Authority and the New Media," *Theory, Culture & Society* 24, no. 2 (2007): 117–34.

18. Wael Hallaq, *An Introduction to Islamic Law* (New York: Cambridge University Press, 2009).

19. Ahram Online, "Egypt's Al-Azhar's Grand Imam Says Islamic Inheritance Law Is 'Not up for Reinterpretation,'" August 21, 2017, http://english.ahram.org.eg/News/275762.aspx.

20. Abou El Fadl, *The Great Theft*, 30.

21. Ed Husain, "The Sunni-Shia Divide," Council on Foreign Relations, 2014, http://www.religionandgeopolitics.org/sectarianism/exploring-sunni-shia-divide.

22. Husain, "The Sunni-Shia Divide."

23. Melani Cammett, "Insight on Syria: A Quagmire of Warring Religious Groups? Why the Western View Is Misguided," Epicenter, September 26, 2017, https://epicenter.wcfia.harvard.edu/blog/insight-syria-quagmire.

24. Nasr Abu Zayd, *Reformation of Islamic Thought: A Critical Historical Analysis* (Amsterdam, Netherlands: Amsterdam University Press, 2006).

25. Abu Zayd, *Reformation of Islamic Thought.*

26. R. Michael Feener and Terenjit Sevea, *Islamic Connections: Muslim Societies in South and Southeast Asia* (Singapore: Institute of Southeast Asian Studies, 2009).

27. Eickelman and Piscatori, *Muslim Politics*, 38.

28. Alexander Horstmann, *Transnational Ideologies and Actors at the Level of Society in South and Southeast Asia* (Washington, DC: National Bureau of Asian Research, 2009).

29. Quintan Wiktorowicz, *Radical Islam Rising: Muslim Extremism in the West* (Boulder, CO: Rowman & Littlefield, 2005).

30. Christine C. Fair et al., "Can Knowledge of Islam Explain Lack of Support for Terrorism? Evidence from Pakistan," *Studies in Conflict and Terrorism* 40, no. 4 (2017): 339–55.

3

How Are Ideologies and Cultures Changing in the Arab World?

THANASSIS CAMBANIS

At the end of the Cold War, many historians and analysts argued that the age of ideology was over—and even more so in the Middle East because of the serial failures of ideologies, whether imported or imposed.[1] But an appraisal of the Middle East today reveals ideology alive at the core of the most dynamic and influential forces at play in the region. The return of ideology is underway worldwide, no less in the Middle East than in Europe and the United States.

Ideology is a unified worldview that molds actions and explains a wide range of phenomena. By nature, ideology is simplifying and to some extent simplistic.[2] Not all politics in the Middle East are ideological, but many of their avatars are. And politics is often inseparable from identity, be it racial, religious, ethnic, or cultural.

Within the Arab world, several ideologies compete. They shape movements and states, conflicts and culture. They are evident in contests for both soft and hard power. Competing ideologies can be seen in the political rhetoric of rival movements, in media and popular culture, and in the ideas that motivate powerful movements. Ideology is every bit as much a factor in the contemporary Middle East as geopolitical interests and patronage politics are.

The most important ideological forces in the region today are Islamism, which has grown somewhat diffuse as it has spread through the region; resistance, exemplified by Iran and Hezbollah; mercantilism, exemplified by Dubai; and military rule, exemplified by Egypt. Some Arab states do not fit easily into any typology, especially those with political systems that allow a wide range of participation. And some ideologies, such as liberalism, have failed to take hold in any serious way, at least on the state level.

53

Like ideological debates in other regions, the Middle East's regional ideologies address questions of how to organize politics, markets, and identity—and they offer their adherents a clear way to understand their place
in the wider world.

Up close, it can be difficult to discern ideological currents. Observers
might see their own environment as free from ideology while dismissing
their opponents as ideologues. Many scholars, without dogmatic intent,
have described the 21st century as a post-ideological age, driven by different factors than the grand ideologies that shaped identity and conflict in
the 20th century.[3] Some Middle Eastern leftists have bemoaned the success of religious ideologies while their own movements have atrophied.

Writing a quarter century ago in *Bitter Legacy*, his study of Arab political
ideology, political scientist Paul Salem concluded that ideology had failed
to achieve the purposes for which it had been mustered and was largely to
blame for the drift in Arab politics.

> After more than seven decades of ideological activity, political
> culture in the Arab world is still in great disarray. There is no
> clear definition of political community, no agreed basis of polit-
> ical legitimacy, no intelligible understanding of political rights
> and duties, no stable framework for political interaction, and
> no widely recognized agenda of political goals. This is a failure
> of ideology in as much as ideology explicitly attempts to resolve
> and provide a foundation for these issues.[4]

What might have been true in 1994 is not, however, the case today. To
be sure, some Arab politicians have operated as opportunists adopting ideology superficially to cling to power or have invoked Islam as a catchall
without crafting a coherent ideology. But others have elaborated a well-
developed worldview.

The region's successful ideologies—as measured by internal coherence,
external power, popularity, and intensity of support—suggest not only that
ideology is alive and well but also that it drives a line of contestation in the
region. Today's Middle East cannot fully be explained by the outside interventions of competing powers and by the internal competition between
Shi'ite and Sunni sectarians or theocrats and secularists. A crucial driver

of regional politics comes from ideological fissures between monarchs and republicans, free-market fundamentalists and central economic planners, proponents of resistance versus those embracing stability, and those who favor military versus civilian rule.

Contemporary Arab history suggests ideology still matters to practical inquiry. First, ideology often drives individual political loyalty and mobilization. Second, ideology plays an indispensable role in the formation of political movements and in political outcomes; ideology is often a pivotal factor that explains motives and choices that cannot be understood by a realist analysis of interests, even one that factors in distortions caused by poor information, misunderstandings, and miscalculation. Third, the governments and other forces that wield power in the Arab world understand their goals and interests embedded in a coherent worldview, which endows a certain edge to convictions.

Today, the term "ideology" is too often used loosely to apply to systems of thought that are perceived as different from the mainstream. So, for example, extremists and fundamentalists are portrayed as motivated by an all-encompassing ideology that gives them greater power but less rigor of thought than reasonable individuals. Another error of analysis is the willingness to define the ideology of movements that achieve tangible political or military power, for example Hezbollah or the Islamic State, while denying or ignoring ideology present in other powerful forces, such as the Gulf Cooperation Council states. Likewise, it is incorrect to suggest that communities such as seculars or nationalists lack ideology simply because they have little political power.

The standard account of contemporary politics holds that interests have trumped ideology as a central motivating factor in the Middle East and elsewhere, as grand ideologies such as communism, liberalism, and Arab nationalism failed to deliver on their promises and gave way to shifting coalitions of interests. The Middle East experienced the supposed end of ideology abruptly after the Arab-Israeli wars of 1967 and 1973. According to this post-ideological account, Middle Eastern leaders and demagogues opportunistically embrace ideology to pursue goals of the moment, but they quickly slough off any ideological imperatives that interfere with their perceived interests.

Under this account, Saudi Arabia, for instance, is a marriage of convenience between a royal family with absolute power and Wahhabi religious extremists who give it legitimacy. There is no Saudi Arabian ideology, *per se*, but rather a ruling family maintaining its power and oil income that can invoke or cast aside the cloak of religious legitimacy borrowed from the Wahhabi establishment as circumstances warrant.

Saddam Hussein rose to power through the Baath Party but during his rule cast aside core elements of its ideology and program and even styled himself as a sort of Islamist late in his rule. Muammar Qadhafi promoted his Third International Theory as an alternative to communism and capitalism and claimed to have invented a new form of democracy in Libya, but in practice he revealed himself to be a standard-issue, if colorful, authoritarian.

Ideology certainly played a central role in Arab politics for a stretch of the 20th century. First, in the early decades of the century, liberalism and its offshoots dominated the political sphere. Then, in the lead-up to World War II and its aftermath, nationalism took over—local nationalisms in places such as Lebanon and Syria, as well as Gamal Abdel Nasser's broader Arab nationalism. After the Arab defeat in the 1967 war with Israel, Islamism emerged as the dominant ideology. But, by the beginning of the 21st century, most political movements had vague ideologies that were almost always superseded by pragmatic tactics and opportunism.

Early in the Arab uprisings of 2010–11, confusion surrounded ideology and politics. Many of the boldest revolutionary movements that briefly resonated with the broader population eschewed politics entirely, instead claiming a mantle of ill-defined reform and change.[5] Labor unions, leftist and anarchist groups, socialist parties, legacy liberal parties, youth movements, and ad hoc revolutionary structures in Egypt and Syria all failed to create coherent ideologies or political programs. In popular politics, Islamists and nationalists dwarfed the small number of revolutionaries, democracy activists, and liberals. The Islamist political space, once legalized in Egypt, emerged as an incoherent spectrum, with rival Salafi and "mainstream" parties and major internal divides over what solutions Islam actually prescribed.

Islamists made impressive gains in elections, prompting many analysts to proclaim an ironclad democratic Islamist majority. Scholars such as Harvard University's Tarek Masoud tried to explain why Islamists were so popular at the ballot box, though drawing conclusions from such a limited number of open elections was problematic.[6] The Brookings Institution's

Shadi Hamid took the analysis a step further by arguing that Islamists had secured the electoral legitimacy to implement an illiberal and undemocratic agenda through the liberal means of the ballot box.[7] These analyses were often premature and could be loose with definitions.

By 2011, the term "Islamism" had come into such wide use, as a self-applied label and as a term of advocacy and research, that it lost almost any specific meaning. While historical roots connected Hamas, Egypt's Muslim Brotherhood, and Tunisia's Ennahda, the three groups had vibrant and distinct ideologies. It would be correct to understand them as ideological movements but false to group them as a single current.

The Islamist space fractured along ideological rather than religious lines, between those who preferred to work within the state and those who sought to topple it. A further divide separated those Islamist political groups that sought to adapt to historical circumstances and those that claimed that, as religious movements, they should not make any compromises.[8]

The left-right ideological divide lost its potency worldwide after the collapse in 1991 of the Soviet Union and the attendant discrediting of communism. Capitalism as an ideology lost its luster after the 2007 global financial crisis. Third Wayism has become the order of the day, ad hoc and incremental. While the grand ideologies of the 20th century were discredited, their heirs have plunged into a contest for hearts and minds in the Middle East.

Four major ideologies are at play in the region: Islamism, resistance, mercantilism, and militarism. They might be noxious to liberals or secularists, and they might appear unsustainable over the long term, but they nonetheless meet the criteria for ideology. Other ideologies—democracy, socialism, and secularism, among others—are in play as well but have been far less successful. Religious movements such as Tunisia's Ennahda, meanwhile, have in some contexts passed into the ideological sphere. Takfiri and jihadi groups, meanwhile, oppose the very system of nation-states and traditional politics, so when they reach power, as the Islamic State did, they explicitly challenge the region's ideological status quo.

The major ideological schools in the Arab world today reflect and shape regional politics and culture. They have built extensive power bases around core ideas and extend their reach into cultural, political, and public life. In most cases, the ideology manifests across national borders, and its most readily identifiable supporters and symbols are not always identical to its sources of hard power or popularity.

All major ideologies invest considerable resources in mobilizing public opinion, through media, popular culture, and, in some cases, the arts. Culture and propaganda merit a study of their own as a battleground for regional ideologies; they form one of the primary points of entry for supporters and potential recruits and also provide branding, ideological definition, and messaging to outsiders and rivals. The cultural and media production of the major schools of ideology often provides the clearest indication of their core beliefs and policy programs.

Of the dominant ideological categories in the Middle East, Islamism has attracted by far the most study and attention. Islamism, loosely defined, includes all those states and movements that claim Islam as the sole source of law and governing legitimacy. Islamists try to construct systems of government or policy platforms based on holy texts.

A wide range of often divergent brands of Islamism have arisen from this broad framework. The Muslim Brotherhood has played a prominent role in Egypt and in the region intermittently since the 1940s. The 1979 Iranian Revolution raised the specter of an Islamist internationally and inspired a variety of movements that sought to radically transform regional politics along religious lines. Jihadi groups have adopted a literalist reading of Islamic jurisprudence and an extremely sectarian worldview.

The resistance axis is articulated in the Arab world by Hezbollah, Lebanon's Party of God, although the theocratic government of Iran provides the underlying ideology, weaponry, and financial resources. The resistance axis originally grew out of Iran's Islamic revolution and has added some accents of its own to the core ideology. It includes the government of Syria and some Iraqi and Palestinian factions. Its core beliefs revolve around what it opposes: Zionism, American foreign policy and hegemony, and the Arab monarchies of the Persian Gulf. Its project is revolutionary and transformative and aspires at its maximum to reorganize society under religious authority and mobilize the public on religious lines.

Mercantilism, meanwhile, is the governing ideology advocated by the rulers of the United Arab Emirates and shared with other Gulf Cooperation Council countries. The monarchs of the Arabian Peninsula have enormous wealth and use a considerable portion of it to proselytize at home and abroad for a system in which absolute rulers provide stability and economic security to a limited number of citizens—and on a conditional basis to guests and residents. Mercantilism encourages limited free enterprise within a broader rentier system. Limited freedoms are allowed away from politics, but only at the rulers' discretion. Residents and citizens forfeit public and civic rights in exchange for a predictably stable environment. This system is conservative and statist, with a preference for a quiescent public.

Militarism is the final ascendant political ideology in today's Middle East, exemplified by the dictatorship of Abdel Fattah el-Sisi in Egypt and reflected in the Bashar al-Assad regime in Syria and "Le Pouvoir," the military alliance that rules Algeria. Militarism as an ideology goes beyond the opportunistic claims of military dictators everywhere. Contemporary militarism suggests that the professional military alone possesses the capacity to govern impartially and effectively and that the military alone embodies the ideas of the people, the nation, and the state. The cult of militarism has deep roots throughout the region; it has permeated Egypt's ruling class and has made inroads in Lebanon, where the military is often described as the lone legitimate national institution.

In practice, this taxonomy is not clean or neat. Even the strongest examples of a single ideology often incorporate elements from other systems of thought. For example, mercantile monarchies in the Gulf embrace Islamism to some degree. Other Arab states defy categorization altogether. Iraq, Lebanon, and Syria host elements of every major ideology, along with small surviving pockets of 20th-century ideologies. Arab nationalism and communism, in particular, left an imprint that extends into the present. Contemporary ideologies draw on the imagined communities and sense of regional interdependence fostered by their ideological predecessors. Projects such as the Iranian Revolution, Zionism, and Kemal Atatürk's secularization of Turkey often factor into Arab ideological debates, whether as a model or a foil.

Statism, with its top-down approach, also runs throughout the region's major ideologies. This statist tradition helps an array of movements justify the subordination of individual liberties and rights to conceptions of collective security and stability, defined by the state.[9] Even those movements that ideologically oppose the traditional state, such as Hezbollah or the Islamic State, seek to replace it with a new centralized authority.

Islamism

Contemporary political Islamism in the Arab world traces its roots to the late-19th-century awakening that spread through the region and spurred some of the early activists and thinkers who espoused a uniquely Islamic solution for politics. By the middle of the 20th century, the most important Islamist group was the Muslim Brotherhood. Originally founded in Egypt, it established branches throughout the region, which coordinated their programs and ideology through an international secretariat. While the Muslim Brotherhood does not self-identify as a Sunni movement in practice, it encapsulates a distinctly Sunni form of Islamism. "Islam is the solution" became a popular slogan, successful at mobilizing group members even if it did not always elucidate alternative policies. Splinter groups articulated the jihadi ideology and evolved into groups such as al Qaeda and Islamic Jihad. Still, the core ideology of the Muslim Brotherhood and its more extremist offshoots remains close to their origins.

Today, the Sunni Islamist political spectrum in the Arab world is broad and heterogeneous. It animates a broad strain of actors, from nihilist jihadi militants in the Sinai Peninsula or the Islamic Group to the Egyptian Muslim Brotherhood to incrementalist mainstream political parties such as Tunisia's Ennahda.

The ideology of the Islamic Republic of Iran runs along a parallel track. Ayatollah Ruhollah Khomeini initially sought to export his revolution and lead Muslims of all sects after he took power in 1979. But a pan-sectarian Islamist revolutionary project never came to fruition, and Iran's Shi'ite Islamism moved in other directions. Domestically, it contended with nationalism, communism, pre-Islamic traditions, and other bodies of belief. Regionally, the Islamic Republic made common cause with an opportunistic group of allies, including the secular state of Syria and Sunni Palestinian militants, leading to shifts that included the creation of resistance ideology.

Islamism is fractured and vague as a political ideology, but it retains distinct hallmarks. Sunni Islamism tends to exacerbate sectarianism and is often intolerant of Muslims of other sects. Islamists promote religion as the source of law and authority and propose states and citizenship schemes that give non-Muslims conditional or limited rights. Similarly, doctrinaire Islamists do not allow for secular, civic, or national conceptions of rights and communities, even when fellow Muslims propose such ideas. Some of the most passionate critics of Islamist ideology are pious Muslims themselves, and they dispute the arguments put forth by varying ideologues who argue that the Quran dictates some uniform political agenda.

Some religious and sectarian parties have started to avoid the label "Islamist." Tunisia's Ennahda Party in 2016 officially dropped its "Islamist" identity to rebrand itself as "Muslim democrats."[10] But the list of Islamist-origin parties and governments in the region is long, and even stoutly anti-Islamist figures owe some portion of their ideology to Islamism. For example, Syria styles itself a secular Baathist republic, and yet the country's constitution stipulates that only a Muslim can serve as president. Such stipulations are common throughout the region, a mark of the reach of Islamist ideas even in states that are primarily not Islamist.

Among the region's ideological currents, extreme jihadi movements have made some of the most visible efforts in the sphere of media and culture. They depend on these spheres not only for recruitment but also to remain relevant even when they lose territory. The Islamic State had a prolific, multilingual media department that published on a wide range of platforms—releasing products as diverse as religious songs, or *nashids*, with music videos, intended to rally followers; Twitter feeds on Islamic jurisprudence; and an English-language magazine called *Inspire*.[11] The Islamic State played a particularly sophisticated role in using pop-culture tools, even releasing a video game.[12] Jihadi groups regularly publish religious circulars, mostly intended for consumption by their followers, which decree each group's permitted dogma. Jihadi groups also release statements and videos for a wider public.

The more mainstream Islamic political groups, such as the Muslim Brotherhood, have been among the least sophisticated on the media and pop-culture front. The Egyptian Muslim Brotherhood's website was awkward and slow.[13] The movement came late to the television game, but now the Brotherhood uses its official Watan television network to mobilize its followers and its unofficial television station, Mekameleen, to irritate the Egyptian government by airing embarrassing leaks.[14]

The Islamic State exhibited the power of Islamic telepreachers living in the West to incite violence and sponsor online radicalization through an established network of extremists, some of whom host their online conferences to defend the group.[15] Still, in the Middle East, telepreaching is no new phenomenon. In Egypt, since the 1970s, preachers have hosted TV programs to discuss and promote Islamic values. Islamic cleric Sheikh Mohamed Mutwali Sharawi, who died in 1998, was an early innovator of televangelism, appealing to university students with his simple vernacular language.[16] Dozens of others have followed this template to spread Islamist teachings through televised sermons.[17]

Resistance

Resistance ideology has recognizable elements of traditional ideologies: a religious foundation, a blueprint for governance, sweeping ambition, a state backer, and a cultish following. Along with Zionism, the ideology of resistance has been one of the most successful political, social, and state-building projects in the modern Middle East, as measured by hard power accrued, followers, and the ability to steer culture and geopolitical events. Resistance ideology has often evolved in explicit opposition to Israeli policy while borrowing techniques of mobilization and state-building from Israel and the Zionist movement.

Iran's 1979 Islamic Revolution brought with it a core idea: *wilayat al faqih*, or guardianship of the jurist, Khomeini's blueprint for clerical rule. Khomeini's treatise spoke directly to questions of legitimacy and governance under Islamic jurisprudence, but it marked only the entry point for the system that emerged under his rule. The Iranian Revolution was religious, radical, and expansionist. Khomeini consolidated power quickly and defined his revolution as much by standing against external forces as he did by advocating a deepening religiosity at home. Revolutionary Iran invested significant resources and political capital to export its ideas around the region, attracting widespread enmity and pushback in states where it intervened.

Resistance relied on a basic formula: religion, militarism, and mobilization against a global enemy and in service of Shi'a ideals. This recipe allowed flexibility. Iran's clerical leaders identified the central enemy as Zionism and US imperialism, but they could add other villains or manipulate their relative emphasis. So too could they emphasize or downplay Shi'ism.

When, for instance, *wilayat al faqih* proved unpopular in Lebanon, Hezbollah simply abandoned it as a practical goal, even as its leaders continued to support the concept in theory. Similarly, Shi'a resistance leaders forged alliances with other sects and marketed themselves as protectors of both minorities and pluralism. The position may be somewhat disingenuous for an authoritarian ideology steeped in Shi'a millenarianism, but it has allowed Iran, Hezbollah, and its ideological allies to contrast themselves with Sunni extremists whose ideology espouses excommunicating or even killing all those it defines as unbelievers.

Like all effective ideologies, resistance has a simple narrative. It has explanatory power and can serve as a guide to action for its followers. During conflict and heightened mobilization, resistance ideology identifies enemies, while at times of peace, resistance ideology invokes a religious-inflected community-building project. In either case, the ideology guides its followers on three planes: It explains events, it gives them a motivation greater than self, and it tells them how to act. And like all effective ideologies, it is adaptable and can withstand the cognitive dissonance that comes from the pursuit of interests that run at odds with the ideology.

For instance, resistance ideology springs from Shi'a ideals of social justice and advocacy for the dispossessed—and yet, since 1979, it has moved to the center of state power. Iran's supreme leader has been in power since 1989. Hezbollah's secretary-general has been in his position since 1992. Both have promoted radical change and transformation across the Middle East and have attacked other leaders as unaccountable, authoritarian, and sectarian, seemingly unaware that they fit the same description.

The partnership between Tehran and Hezbollah anchors the resistance axis; it is a coalition of affinity and interests. An analysis of Hezbollah as an Iranian proxy misses the partnership's normative and ideological dimensions. Hezbollah was actively created by Iran's Islamic Revolutionary Guard Corps, out of preexisting indigenous Lebanese organizations.[18] The result was a like-minded and adaptive organization cut of the same cloth as its parent.

In the Arab world, Hezbollah's resistance ideology has become a formidable transnational force. The group projects hard power through its interventions in Iraq, Syria, and Yemen. Hezbollah's ideas, rhetoric, and governance also serve as a model for some actors in these countries. Hezbollah has been blamed for populist and Shi'a sectarian initiatives around the region. Bahraini activists and Hamas militants have both modeled aspects of their programs and activities on Lebanese Hezbollah, which has also spurred direct copycat movements in Iraq and Syria.

Hezbollah's followers in Lebanon follow the explications of their leaders, especially during times of crisis. Unlike communities whose loyalty is passive, Hezbollah demands commitment and sacrifice from its loyalists and takes care to elicit buy-in for its policies, sometimes admitting mistakes and other times weaving tortured conspiracy theories. Examples abound, including the lengthy speeches that Hassan Nasrallah made during the 2006 war that gradually won over some critics and his apology for miscalculating the scope of Israel's response to the intellectually labored support for Arab uprisings unless they challenge Hezbollah's authoritarian allies. At the same time, the concrete backing the movement enjoys makes it a force with which to be reckoned.

Hezbollah's intervention in Syria highlights the interplay of interests and ideology. Like Iran, Hezbollah saw a strategic imperative to prop up the government in Damascus. Yet, Hezbollah could not embark on a full-fledged war in Syria without its constituency's consent. Nasrallah set out building the case for that intervention early in the Syrian uprising and continued the discussion long after Hezbollah's undeclared military activities inside Syria had become an open secret. His followers excused the lie because they believed that a vast outside conspiracy threatened their freedom and religion. All means were justified in its defense.

Hezbollah's ideological vigor is one strand among many. Unlike other movements, Hezbollah observes no boundaries between its community and leadership, its ideas and practice, and its army and ideas. Leaders suffer the same consequences as rank-and-file supporters, including destruction of their homes during conflict and the death of children who have enlisted to fight for the resistance. Ideology reinforces unity of purpose. Always mobilized and always attuned to global politics, Hezbollah addresses criticism. When it denies evidence or lies, it does so unapologetically, just as it does when it extols the sacrifices of its community.

Hezbollah officials never shy away from thanking Iran, Syria, and other patrons. Nor do they avoid talking about the willingness of Hezbollah supporters to face death. Sacrifice is no less important than the narrative woven around it, which amplifies Hezbollah's power as a movement not of interests but of "loyalty to the resistance," not by coincidence the name the party's parliamentary bloc adopted. Addressing a gathering of international operatives supporting the "Islamic Resistance," Nasrallah spoke at length about the factors that enabled Hezbollah to withstand pressure from richer and better armed enemies.

> One of the main elements of strength of any resistance is its popular embrace and environment—the people who support this resistance and back it and offer it their children, and hold the funerals of its martyrs with pride, and show tolerance when they are wounded and when their houses are destroyed, and when their fortunes are being blazed down. They tolerate displacement and do not harm the resistance with a word. They rather support it with all their strength and back it to be able to proceed.[19]

Looking back on the 2006 war a decade later, Nasrallah observed:

> We entered the era of victories, and the time of defeats has come to an end. . . . [The United States and its allies] did everything they can do: sectarian sedition, factional sedition, money, suicide attackers, and gathering the savage beasts from around the world. Here their project is collapsing. This scheme has no prospects for the future. The future of Lebanon is the Resistance, the future of Palestine is the Resistance, and the future of Syria is the Resistance. The future of the region is the future of our peoples and our nation and its dignity, pride, and sovereignty. Peace be upon you and Allah's mercy and blessings.[20]

Notice the ingredients: triumphalism; an inexhaustible enemy front that connects al Qaeda, Israel, and the United States, among others, in a conspiracy against Hezbollah's resistance front; transnational unity; and a powerful community rooted in individuals' loyalty. Conveniently, neither stability nor conventional military victories are necessary. Economic prosperity and services burnish Hezbollah's appeal but are not strictly necessary for its communal support. Its willingness to destabilize other states and operate in anarchic zones with multiple power centers makes it a formidable adversary. Its recipe of community building plus armed militancy endows its model with wide appeal.

The resistance axis has prioritized social mobilization since its early years, investing in public art, public spectacles, documentary films, and cultural programming, along with news and music, as vectors of ideological formation.[21] Hezbollah offers a rich example. Its Al Manar television channel and Al Nour radio offer strictly controlled official news and programming, including children's shows and religious education. For example, Al Manar features a children's segment called "Stories for Children" that shows cartoon stories of the lives of the prophets in Islam and animated narratives on the Battle of Karbala and the history of the Shi'a.[22] Al Manar plays a huge role in creating a narrative of its enemy's history and demeanor. In 2003, it aired the controversial Syrian dramatic TV series *Al Shattat* ("The Diaspora"). The series claims to present a historical view of Zionism and anti-Semitism and paints a picture of the Jew as murderer and conspirator.[23] Hezbollah has also used poetry written by its own members as a mobilizing medium of expression.[24]

Private channels not directly under Hezbollah's official control offer more freewheeling resistance programming that never deviates from the official line; an example is Al Mayadeen. Websites collect resistance documentation, including political speeches, heroic war stories, and tributes to martyrs.[25] Even further, the popularity of "the resistance" permeates the popular music scene. In Lebanon, Julia Boutros, a giant in the music industry, includes tribute songs in her albums especially for Hezbollah and Nasrallah.[26] Mobilizing tools through media, popular culture, and the arts reconstruct narratives and travel beyond a movement's official channels and platforms.[27]

Mercantilism

The oil-rich Arab monarchies of the Persian Gulf have embraced the ideology of mercantilism. The royal family demands absolute authority but grants a limited number of citizens the right to prosperity. Cut through reams of public relations documents, and this is the ideology at the heart of the "Dubai model."

The system offers a zone where citizens and various tiers of guests may partake in a profitable economy, on terms dictated by the ruling family. Business is treated more or less fairly. The system's goal is to increase wealth, with first priority always given to the rulers' share, and to eliminate social and political friction through a heavily regulated environment.

The offer at the core of this system is attractive to many: Follow the rules of the royal family, and live with security, consistency, and, in most cases, relative prosperity. As a result, hundreds of thousands of Middle Easterners have flocked to the oil-rich Arab kingdoms since the 1970s. There is no right to political or cultural freedom, even if the ruling family's attitudes change with time. The rules are informal and not always articulated; when they change, there is no recourse or appeal.

The mercantile model offers an oasis of relative calm. Authoritarian bargains characterize rule everywhere in the region, from relatively liberal Lebanon, Morocco, and Tunisia to more blunt and heavy-handed dictatorships such as Algeria, Egypt, Iran, and Saudi Arabia. What distinguishes the mercantilist model is its willingness to allow creative space for entrepreneurs and even some politicians, artists, and cultural figures—so long as their exertions do not offend the rulers' values or trespass against their interests.

Filmmaker and poet Hind Shoufani identified the unique position of Dubai as a comparatively open Arab city in 2013. She had lived there for four years at the time. Compared to other cities she had called home, including Beirut, Damascus, and New York, Shoufani said Dubai offered steady, secure work in an Arab environment that functioned smoothly with clear rules.

> Yes, it's a bubble—but who's to say we should be living in a horrible environment all the time. Why? . . . There is a certain respect for creating in Dubai—because people are from all

over the world, they are exposed to culture. They know how to respect culture. As long as we don't go out of our way to offend the sheikhs, we're fine.[28]

The rulers of the Emirates have created a model that Bahrain, Kuwait, Oman, and Qatar have followed to some degree. Saudi Arabia appears to be adopting some aspects of the ideological template within enclaves.

For the Gulf monarchs, the system works. Not only have they survived, but they have grown rich without the complications faced by rulers balancing more representative systems. But is the mercantilist approach solely the result of vast wealth? Gulf monarchies are steeped in more religious and tribal traditions than the urban ruling class in the Levant and Maghreb.[29] In modern times, however, the Gulf rulers have paid careful attention to ideological cleavages and economic exigencies. As petro-states, they have sought to manage oil rents and plan for a post-oil future. As absolute monarchies with a conservative, even reactionary citizenry and a vast population of guest workers, they have sought to manage ideological ferment.

Some Gulf rulers simply tried to mold regional currents, supporting a bedeviling array of Salafist clerics, jihadi militants, and Muslim Brothers at various periods in bids to control or co-opt religious challenges. Over time, however, the shrewdest leaders in the Gulf built and articulated an alternative of their own: the quietist, traditional Sunni Arab monarchy, with surface tolerance and elasticity but a hard, conservative authoritarian bedrock. Dubai's mercantile model preserves a sense of Arab and Muslim cultural identity in an environment conducive to business but less so to culture and hostile to politics and dissent. The Gulf ideology has won adherents from the wider Arab and non-Arab world as a result of its obsession with achievement, taking top billing on elements such as hotels, malls, and airports, and Arabizing fields dominated by non-Arab achievement. It offers a version of Beirut with the brouhaha and bombs, pluralism without rights.

In a region rife with armed conflict, stagnation, poverty, and radicalism, the city-states of the United Arab Emirates offer an alternative three-part formula: first, an ideology and identity; second, governance that works; and third, economic opportunity. Here is Sheikh Maktoum of Dubai, explaining the formula in September 2014, when the Islamic State was at its apogee:

Only one thing can stop a suicidal youth who is ready to die for ISIS: a stronger ideology that guides him onto the right path and convinces him that God created us to improve our world, not to destroy it. . . . When governments fail to address instability, legitimate grievances, and persistent serious challenges, they create an ideal environment for hateful ideologies to incubate—and for terrorist organizations to fill the vacuum of legitimacy.[30]

The mercantilist ideologues are willing to spend money propagating their ideology throughout the region. Increasingly, they are willing to deploy military power, diplomacy, and financial investments on behalf of their school of thought.[31] For example, when the Emirates and Saudi Arabia accelerated their confrontational policy toward Iran and rift with Qatar in 2017, they were willing to harm their own short-term economic interests.

In spats with Iran, Gulf countries have expelled or threatened to expel residents with Lebanese nationality and Shi'a origin as alleged Hezbollah fifth columnists.[32] The decision was arbitrary and had no evidentiary basis; the expelled workers were not individuals identified by law enforcement as having Hezbollah ties or engaging in illegal activity. Yet the expulsion had a specific purpose: to remind guests in the mercantile Gulf that in the eyes of the government, they had no rights—only privileges and responsibilities. Their permission to participate in the Gulf's economic boom was solely at the pleasure of the royal family.

A more ambiguous example is Saudi Arabia, which has kept the mercantile experiment at arm's length but has invested heavily in its relationship with the Emirates and now seems willing to adopt some of the Emirates' approaches. For several decades, Saudi Arabia has experimented with ways to diversify its oil economy and improve its domestic labor force to reduce its dependency on foreign labor. The kingdom has courted foreign investment; opened universities and economic zones operating under special, more liberal laws; and lifted some restrictions (on access to entertainment and women's mobility, for example) while insisting that Saudi Arabia maintains its traditional bedrock character as the guardian of Islam.

These efforts were halting and had little impact until 2015, when the new king put his young son, Prince Mohammed bin Salman, effectively in charge of the kingdom. Mohammed bin Salman radically changed decision-making within the royal family and has accelerated shifts in financial flows and economic policy. Mohammed bin Salman can sound like a cross between *A Thousand and One Nights* and a Silicon Valley startup pitch, as when he asserted that Neom, his proposed new megacity on the Red Sea, "represents a civilizational leap for all humanity."[33] He enumerated some madcap ideas to reporters during a carefully choreographed rollout of new policies in October 2017. "We want the main robot and the first robot in Neom to be Neom itself," the crown prince said. "Robot number one. Everything will have a link to artificial intelligence, to the Internet of Things—everything."[34] These are not the comical musings of an absolute but unhinged monarch; they are markers of the mercantile ideology, as practiced by an enormously powerful head of state.

Modern Gulf mercantilism has elements of the traditional authoritarian bargain—social welfare in exchange for a suspension of politics and rights—but it goes far beyond that. The monarchs articulate a basket of affirmatives: Arab achievement, tradition, economic opportunity, stability, and a relatively nonviolent and noncoercive form of authoritarianism, in which dissidents and critics are more likely to be deported, co-opted, or detained for a limited term than to be tortured, killed, or detained indefinitely, as is the norm in the region's police states. This combination of inducements has made the mercantilist model a strong performer in the region's ideological contest, as evinced by the great number of outsiders who voluntarily move to the Gulf and subordinate themselves to its ideology.

With their eye for slick marketing and long-term investments, the Arab Gulf states pioneered modern news and entertainment programming as a vehicle of soft power. Qatar broke the model of state news monopolies with the foundation of Al Jazeera in 1996.[35] In the decades since, all the Gulf monarchies, but especially the United Arab Emirates and Saudi Arabia, have invested in a full spectrum of satellite television networks. They also have established their own production companies and invested in others.

The result is a suite of products, including advertisements, music videos, original entertainment programming, stations that air films and independently produced shows from all over the world, didactic talk shows, and professionally produced news. Some of these platforms directly extend the Gulf ideology and priorities of their state sponsors.

Other platforms, such as the music videos and ads produced in the Gulf and aired on their networks, indirectly promote the mercantilist model: high production values; a rainbow coalition of Middle Easterners thriving together in a prosperous, apolitical framework; and openness to culture from the Arab world, the West, and the East.

The Emirates have invested in an expansion of conglomerates such as Middle East Broadcasting Center and other entertainment and advertising companies in Dubai Media City. The government also has successfully catalyzed a booming art and media scene that has changed the look and feel of Gulf states.[36]

For Emirati nationals, this dynamism can accentuate pride in the formula whereby their country has developed without abandoning its traditional values and ruling bargain.[37] That bargain is evident in shows such as *Hams Al Hareer* ("The Whisper of Silk"), which portrays a modern Emirati women successfully balancing a career with her role as a mother and wife.[38] Another program, *Shababouna* ("Our Youth"), encourages Emirati youth to take an active role in the country's economy.[39] Other programs, such as the documentary *Hayati al-Askariyya* ("My Military Life"), promote a form of nationalism through their portrayals of "the lives of a few brave and devoted UAE Armed Forces personnel, in a country blessed with peace and security."[40]

A 2017 Ramadan public service video from the Kuwaiti telecoms company Zain achieved a high-water mark of the mercantile ideology's packaging of politics, entertainment, religion, and commerce. It featured an actor playing a suicide bomber, whose fanatical chants are slowly overtaken by the singing of a smiling crowd representing an array of Middle Eastern archetypes. Love and open-minded religion conquers fundamentalism. The clip climaxes with the Emirati pop star Hussein Al Jasmi singing that people should worship God with love and not with terror.[41] The three-minute video went viral.

Military Rule as End, Not Means

Military rule in Egypt has distinguished itself with an effort to build an ideology beyond the exigencies shared by any dictatorship. Since the Egyptian popular uprisings of 2011, the military has steadily eliminated traditional political space while simultaneously drafting a ruling ideology. Its goal is to legitimize military rule, forestall challenges to its legitimacy, mobilize the population away from political engagement and into nation-building exercises that encourage passive obedience to the authorities, and finally, redefine the concepts of nation, state, and people as subsidiaries of the military, which is not only the institutional but also the spiritual trustee of all three. This carefully designed ideology lays the groundwork for authoritarianism and also for a cult of absolute rule that no longer depends on the individual personality of the official in charge. Sisi, a general who spent the formative years of his career in military intelligence, has been instrumental in designing Egypt's new militarism.

Sisi came to power against the backdrop of a military coup. On July 3, 2013, he deposed President Mohamed Morsi. A month later he used force to kill upward of 1,000 Morsi supporters. Military leaders embraced a simple mantra: stability or chaos. Over time, they built the case that every other institution and individual had failed to bring stability to Egypt; only the military remained. By the time of the coup, Sisi had drafted a cadre of politicians, secular and Islamist, along with youth leaders and clerics, who publicly asked the military to intervene in politics. During the subsequent transition period, Sisi retired from the military and then allowed himself to be "drafted" as a civilian for service. One-time revolutionaries celebrated the new dictatorship as a military solution to an intractable political problem. When critics and foreign governments called it a coup, Sisi's supporters responded their "revolution" was at the very least a "popularly legitimate coup."

Ideological projects are measured by different criteria than retail politics. The new militaristic regime will not face meaningful challenges at the ballot box—it controls the process—and moreover, if Sisi fails individually, he can be replaced by another member of the Supreme Council of the Armed Forces, whom elections can duly anoint. Public buy-in for the new militaristic Egypt might be coerced, but it is significant and growing.

Contemporary Egyptian militarism, as crafted by Sisi, has several distinguishing features. It subsumes existing threads of Egyptian and pan-Arab nationalism under chauvinist patriotism. Sisi rallies the public and the institutions of state around an endless cycle of grandiose nation-building projects, such as a second Suez Canal and a new capital city, which endowed

Egypt's new military rule with a grand sense of purpose and accomplishment. They have been followed by other grand gestures, some of them significant, such as the devaluation of Egypt's currency and the partial elimination of historically untouchable subsidies to bread and energy. In this calculation, it does not matter whether the projects actually work; what matters is that military rule is established as more daring, capable, effective, and truly Egyptian than other alternatives.

The militarist ideology demands compliance from the citizenry. While resistance society requires active buy-in and sacrifice from members, the militarist state demands passive loyalty through quiescence and obedience.

Finally, the ideology paints the military not simply as the guardian of national values and security, but as their very embodiment: The military does not simply protect Egypt; it *is* Egypt. The same syllogism holds for other key concepts. The military becomes synonymous with the people, the state, the nation, national security, and so forth.

Since coming to power, Sisi's regime has spent much of its time repressing its citizenry to an unprecedented degree, even compared to Egypt's previous dictatorships. His government has detained 60,000 political prisoners, shut down public spaces that had relative freedom under all previous dictatorships dating back to the end of colonial rule, and engaged in an ever-widening gyre of crackdowns against anyone who does not toe the regime's line, including potential rivals inside the military and loyal elite, political activists, and gay rights–sympathizing concertgoers. But these acts of repression, in tandem with efforts to erase the history of the 2011–13 revolutionary period, should not obscure the regime's ongoing and successful efforts to create an alternate ideology.

Sisi's praetorian state presents itself as a military regime rather than the purview of one man. The fault of Mubarak's dictatorship was not its governance failures, in this analysis, but its substitution of a dynastic family for the state. Sisi's rhetoric, and his actions so far, suggest that he is a true believer in military rule; he has placed an ever-greater share of the national economy and state under the control of generals, active duty and retired. The competence of military officers to run a huge state has been lacking, even as measured by their civil servant predecessors. But all oversight and democratic accountability have been crushed by the authoritarian state, so it has been free to build its ideology without any significant challenge.

Ideologies compete. Within the first minute of his speech inaugurating the Suez Canal, Sisi announced another initiative: to restore Egypt's position as a moderate leader of Islam.

> Allow me to talk to you as an Egyptian citizen who takes pride in the magnificence of his country and ancient civilization, which is taught around the world so that the peoples of the world take inspiration from the values it espoused. And today Egypt presents its gift to the world for the sake of humanity, reconstruction and development. Over the last two years, Egypt's contributions to the world have extended beyond this new canal, to encompass other vital areas. History will judge that Egypt and its people confronted the most dangerous, extremist, terrorist thinking, which, had it prevailed, would have set the world ablaze.[42]

While cynics have much ground for their criticism, in Sisi's telling, Egypt's actions had saved the world from the fire of jihadi terrorism. This rhetoric might sound hollow, but it serves a key function in ideological consolidation. As writer Sarah Carr put it in her biting dispatch from the Suez Canal opening:

> This is a regime of grand gestures (is there any more grand a gesture than removing a president from power?) that has so far made little inroads on Egypt's multifarious and intractable socioeconomic problems while it continues to tighten the noose on civil liberties, with apparent widespread public support. Grand gestures are always a gamble. This one seems to have paid off—at least for now.[43]

Successful ideological regimes need popular consent, so in militaristic Egypt, the state choreographs consent. The state values public shows of loyalty and lays the groundwork to make sure that those public displays feed the regime's ideology: the military first, as guardian of the people and restorer of greatness.

Throughout the fall after the coup, Egyptian media of all stripes—private and public, television and radio—gave constant airtime to a song of praise about the army called "Blessed Be the Hands."⁴⁴ The ballad emerged as a spontaneous thank-you to Sisi and ended up six months later as his presidential campaign song. Its lyrics portray Egyptian military men as embodying self-sacrifice and most conceivable virtues in the service of the people and the nation and depicts the military as coming to Egypt's rescue at the request of the Egyptian people. Military rule is portrayed as a sacrifice that the Egyptian military is willing to make—but only because the people ask for it so insistently.

While the claim is self-serving fiction, it has created a logic for the military as the representative of the Egyptian public. Some of this approach borrows heavily from Nasserism, which portrayed a military coup as a popular revolution in 1952 and which simultaneously delivered popular policy reforms while stifling public life and shutting down politics entirely.⁴⁵

The United Arab Emirates and Saudi Arabia have provided the crucial financial support to keep the new military regime in power, even though so much about Egypt's ideology and identity amount to a rebuke to the ideology of the mercantile monarchy. Egypt is a republic of citizens, and it runs today on a militaristic populist ideology that draws on a distinct, chauvinist Egyptian identity with ancient roots. While the Emirates and Egypt share a distaste for the Muslim Brotherhood, they each consider their own brand of state-supported, tolerant Islam the correct blueprint for the region.

Egypt's new, or renewed, praetorian ideology has significantly affected Egypt itself and serves as a third example of a coherent state ideology in the region, although for now it is the only military-republic of its type on the horizon. Libya's strongman contender Khalifa Haftar has expressed similar views and could conceivably try to create a similar type of regime were he ever to rule Libya. Now safely ensconced in power, Sisi and the generals who run Egypt have continued building an ideology-centered regime, with pretensions of regional impact. Egypt is certainly less influential and powerful than its present-day leaders imagine, but it has not entirely lost its importance in the Arab world.

The Gulf's well-financed news media and entertainment industry has overtaken Egypt's for influence and audience in the Arab world. But Egypt's news and entertainment complex remains prolific, with a domestic audience of more than 90 million.

The Egyptian government has always relied on media, culture, and propaganda to spread its ideology, traditionally through a mix of indirect pressure, censorship, and coercion. Sisi's regime has gone to greater lengths
than its predecessors to choreograph consent and stifle space for free
expression. While it has exhibited less tolerance for criticism than previous dictatorships, its approach has been consistent with historical use of
Egypt's cultural and media sphere to promote ideology.

State-owned media dominates the landscape, including daily newspapers, weeklies, and television channels. Its editors are selected by the
government and closely monitored.[46] Privately owned television and
newspapers occasionally push boundaries, both in style and content, and
are often more popular because of their higher production values. But
state intelligence still carefully manages the content of media and cultural
platforms that are not directly under state control.

State control eliminates dissenting views and, equally importantly, promotes the state's nationalist and militarist ideology, emphasizing national
unity and the sanctity of the military's role.[47] Broadcasters openly promote
the state's ideological agenda. One particularly vivid (and disturbing)
example came in 2014, when a camera crew accompanied a police raid on
an alleged gay bathhouse and aired footage of the arrests, accompanied by
praise from the program host.[48] The raid and broadcast signaled the beginning of a new round of state persecution of gay Egyptians.

Sour notes are quickly silenced from public and private networks
and forums. For example, the government pressured a private network
in 2014 to cancel Bassem Youssef's popular satirical show *Al-Bernameg*
("The Program").[49] Liliane Daoud, a British-Lebanese presenter at the private ONTV station, was deported in June 2016 after the network termi-
nated her contract.[50]

Popular culture (film, song, drama series, and graffiti) shapes and at
times destabilizes people's perceptions of the army. When Sisi came to
power, the new military regime dominated the cultural field and promoted
a personality cult connecting the new leader to the 2011 revolution, packaging him as "*savior, military leader, hero* and *father* for all Egyptians."[51]
In culture and media, the military ideology presents itself as a unified
embodiment of several dissonant currents: popular revolution, national
resilience, military prowess, and peace through strength.

Conclusion: Political and Cultural Struggle

The newer ideologies of resistance, mercantile monarchy, and militarism, like Islamism before them, will carve out increasingly important platforms across the region. Factors such as popular revolt, reform, conflict, or foreign intervention could bring other ideologies to the fore. Legacy ideologies, including Nasserism, communism, Baathism, and nationalisms, including pan-Arab nationalism and local nationalist movements such as the Syrian Social Nationalist Party, all continue to play important roles, holding power or wielding influence in various loci of power. Islamism might once again play a central role in the region's ideological development, as it has repeatedly since the 1970s, or it might spawn other distinct ideological offspring movements. Similarly, some of the secular, anti-sectarian, democratic, and liberal ideologies that have persisted since at least the early 20th century command pockets of influence.

The generation that followed the end of the Cold War was characterized worldwide by ideological drift. After communism and capitalism dominated Western consciousness, it was hard to discern which ideas, if any, would sway in the aftermath of one stifling debate. Similarly, in the Arab world, the grand ideologies that fed the Arab Cold War were discredited by practical failures—first of governance and, fatally, of fundamental competence, as evinced by Israel's military defeat of Arab armies in 1967. Today's ideologies emerged from the long fallow period that followed, during which a widespread but vague Islamist cloak seemed to be the only dynamic source of ideology but during which states experimented with other constructs.

Today's big three ideologies are road tested and have emerged as ideas rooted in durable power centers. Their prospects differ, however. Resistance and monarchical mercantilism both possess the potential for long-term influence. They have powerful state sponsors, with institutional capacity, the financial wherewithal that comes with energy reserves, and viable social identities with which their adherents can identify. The resistance and burgeoning mercantilist blocs have also demonstrated a capacity to deliver governance and security via state or state-like institutions.

Militarism's long-term prospects are shakier. Its ideological core draws heavily on Arab nationalism, and as such, it risks being similarly brittle. So far, Egypt's military state has fared poorly at governance and security. Its propaganda and cultural construction are blunt, preoccupied as much with stifling alternative narratives as with constructing a new affirmative one. Of the three strong ideologies at play in the Arab world, it is structurally the weakest.

For all the talk of a post-ideological age, the future of public opinion in the Middle East is being contested on ideological grounds. Regional powers are engaged in cultural, media, and religious wars, along with open and proxy conflicts. As acutely as in any region—perhaps more so, judging by the proliferation of satellite channels and the money invested in ideologically motivated conflict—Arab ideologues are hard at work articulating their ideologies and seeking adherents. The centrality of this contest is evident in music production, television talk shows, entertainment serials, and the widespread network of state-funded religious and social organizations with a proselytizing element. Many of the region's proxy wars reflect and embody ideological cleavages. The hot wars that have savaged Iraq, Libya, Syria, and Yemen all contain ideological fissures and have invited intervention by regional powers preoccupied with consolidating influence and propping up their ideological model. The contest among resistance, mercantilism, and militarism manifests to a certain degree in almost every one of the Arab world's ongoing civil conflicts.

As these ideological states mature in power, they will articulate their views more confidently and clearly, just as they already have begun to pursue their material interests more aggressively. Another age of ideology has dawned.

Notes

1. See Francis Fukuyama, *The End of History and the Last Man* (New York: Simon and Schuster, 1992); Daniel Bell, *The End of Ideology: On the Exhaustion of Political Ideas in the Fifties* (Cambridge, MA: Harvard University Press, 1960); Seymour Martin Lipset, *Political Man: The Social Bases of Politics* (Garden City, NY: Doubleday, 1960); Ghassan Salame, "Inter-Arab Politics: The Return of Geography," in *The Middle East: Ten Years After Camp David*, ed. William B. Quandt (Washington, DC: Brookings Institution, 1988); Paul Salem, *Bitter Legacy: Ideology and Politics in the Arab World* (New York: Syracuse University Press, 1994); Bassel F. Salloukh, "Studying Arab Politics: The End of Ideology or the Quest for Alternative Methods?," *Critique: Critique Middle Eastern Studies* 6, no. 10 (1997): 109–25; and Michael Hudson, *Arab Politics: The Search for Legitimacy* (New Haven, CT: Yale University Press, 1979).

2. Salem, *Bitter Legacy*, 3.

3. See the debate on ideology in the post-ideological age in Slavoj Žižek, ed., *Mapping Ideology* (London, New York: Verso, 1994). Also see the debate among the philosophy of Hurgen Habermas, Michel Foucault, and Žižek ideology in Saul Newman, *Power and Politics in Poststructuralist Thought: New Theories of the Political* (New York: Routledge, 2005), 73–81.

4. Salem, *Bitter Legacy*, 262.

5. Athanasios Cambanis, *Once Upon a Revolution: An Egyptian Story* (New York: Simon & Schuster, 2015).

6. Tarek Masoud, *Counting Islam: Religion, Class, and Elections in Egypt* (New York: Cambridge University Press, 2014).

7. Shadi Hamid, *Islamic Exceptionalism: How the Struggle over Islam Is Reshaping the World* (New York: St. Martin's Press, 2016).

8. Olivier Roy, "Political Islam After the Arab Spring: Between Jihad and Democracy," *Foreign Affairs*, November/December 2017, https://www.foreignaffairs.com/reviews/review-essay/2017-10-16/political-islam-after-arab-spring.

9. Michael Wahid Hanna, "Public Order and Egypt's Statist Tradition," *Review of Faith & International Affairs* 13, no. 1 (2015): 23–30.

10. Heba Saleh, "Tunisia's Nahda Party Ditches Islamist Tag," *Financial Times*, May 22, 2016, https://www.ft.com/content/966407b8-2033-11e6-aa98-db1e01fabc0c.

11. Charlie Winter, *Documenting the Virtual "Caliphate,"* Quilliam, 2015, http://www.quilliaminternational.com/wp-content/uploads/2015/10/FINAL-documenting-the-virtual-caliphate.pdf.

12. Brendan I. Koerner, "Why ISIS Is Winning the Social Media War," *Wired*, 2016, https://www.wired.com/2016/03/isis-winning-social-media-war-heres-beat/.

13. The Egyptian Muslim Brotherhood's official website is http://www.ikhwanonline.com/ [Arabic] and http://www.ikhwanweb.com/ [English].

14. Watan TV, http://www.watanegypt.tv/; and Mekameleen, http://www.mekameleen.net/.

80 SEVEN PILLARS

15. Lizzie Deardon, "London Attack Linked to Hate Preacher Anjem Choudary's Extremist Network," Independent, June 6, 2017, http://www.independent.co.uk/news/uk/home-news/london-attack-bridge-borough-isis-perpetrators-khuram-butt-links-anjem-choudary-documentary-jihadis-a7776101.html; and Shiv Malek, "Radical Preachers Praise Isis in Online Conference," Guardian, September 8, 2014, https://www.theguardian.com/uk-news/2014/sep/08/radical-preachers-isis-islamic-state-online-conference.

16. Adel Darwish, "Obituary: Sheikh Mohamed Mutwali Sharawi," Independent, June 18, 1998, http://www.independent.co.uk/arts-entertainment/obituary-sheikh-'mohamed-mutwali-sharawi-1165880.html; and Yasmin Moll, "Islamic Satellite Channels and the Ethics of Entertainment in Egypt," Carnegie Endowment for International Peace, April 21, 2010, https://carnegieendowment.org/sada/40646.

17. Nermeen Alazrak and Alamira Samah Saleh, "The Neo-Liberal Islamic Preachers: 'It Is Not Enough to Believe, but You Must Act on Your Faith,'" in Political Islam and Global Media: The Boundaries of Religious Identity, ed. Noha Mellor and Khalil Rinnawi (Abingdon, UK: Routledge, 2016), 219–31.

18. See Augustus Richard Norton, Hezbollah: A Short History (Princeton, NJ: Princeton University Press, 2007); Augustus Richard Norton, Amal and the Shi'a: Struggle for the Soul of Lebanon (Austin, TX: University of Texas Press, 1987); Judith Palmer Harik, Hezbollah: The Changing Face of Terrorism (London: I. B. Tauris, 2005); and, for the narrative from Hezbollah's own perspective, Na'īm Qāsim, Hizbullah (Hezbollah): The Story from Within (London: Saqi Books, 2010).

19. Hassan Nasrallah, "Sayyed Nasrallah's Full Speech on the Islamic Resistance Support Organization Honorary Ceremony (Part 1)," Alahed News, May 6, 2016, https://english.alahednews.com.lb/essaydetails.php?eid=33345&cid=570#.WfLYRBOCyV4.

20. Hassan Nasrallah, "Full Speech Delivered by Hizbullah Secretary General, His Eminence Sayyed Nasrallah, on the Divine Victory Anniversary Ceremony Held in Bint Jbeil on August 13, 2016," Alahed News, https://english.alahednews.com.lb/essaydetails.php?eid=34603&cid=570#.WfLYNxOCyV4.

21. Amal Saad-Ghorayeb, Hizbu'llah: Politics and Religion (London: Pluto Press, 2002); and Phillip Smyth, "Jihadology: Hizbullah Cavalcade," Jihadology, http://jihadology.net/hizballah-cavalcade/.

22. ShiaTV, "[1/4] Hazrat Abbas Martyrdom Karbala | Al-Manar | Stories for Children—Arabic," https://www.shiatv.net/video/452939213; and Forthe Mahdi, "Prophet Saleh (as)—FULL | Al-Manar | Eng Subs | Stories for Children," YouTube, 32:01, April 6, 2015, https://www.youtube.com/watch?v=NuFri8No8WI.

23. Reese Schonfeld, "The Global Battle for Cultural Domination," in Developing Cultures: Essays on Cultural Change, ed. Lawrence E. Harrison and Jerome Kagan (Abingdon, UK: Routledge, 2006), 309–11.

24. Atef Alshaer, Poetry and Politics in the Modern Arab World (London: C. Hurst and Co., 2016).

25. War Media Center, Twitter, https://twitter.com/C_Military1; Al Manar TV, http://english.almanar.com.lb/; Hassan Nasrallah, Al Manar TV, https://english.almanar.com.lb/cat/news/lebanon/s-nasrallah-speeches; Al Nour Radio, http://www.alnour.com.lb/; Alahed News, https://www.alahednews.com.lb/; Electronic Resistance, Twitter, https://

twitter.com/resistanceer?lang=en; Janoubia, http://janoubia.com/; and Al Mayadeen TV, http://www.almayadeen.net/

26. See Jamericu, "Julia Boutros Ahibaii Video Clip Hezbollah Nasrallah," You-Tube, 4:57, September 16, 2007, https://www.youtube.com/watch?v=uTdEAm3WhmA; and Monitor Mideast, "Christian Singer Honors Hezbollah in Stunning 2013 Concert Performance," YouTube, 8:13, September 8, 2013, https://www.youtube.com/watch?v=pdZgkGI5hoA.

27. See Bashir Saade, *Hizbullah and the Politics of Remembrance: Writing the Lebanese Nation* (Cambridge, UK: Cambridge University Press, 2016); and Zahera Harb, *Channels of Resistance in Lebanon: Liberation Propaganda, Hezbollah and the Media* (London: I. B. Tauris, 2011).

28. Hind Shoufani, in discussion with the author, November 2013.

29. Yasser Elsheshtawy, "Tribes with Cities," Dubaization, November 5, 2013, https://dubaization.com/post/66097171299/tribes-with-cities.

30. Mohammed bin Rashid al Maktoum, "The Intellectual Battle Against ISIS," Project Syndicate, September 27, 2014, https://www.project-syndicate.org/commentary/mohammed-bin-rashid-al-maktoum-calls-for-a-broad-development-agenda-to-defeat-the-middle-east-s-ideologies-of-hate.

31. Michael Stephens, "The Arab Cold War Redux: The Foreign Policy of the Gulf Cooperation Council States Since 2011," in *Arab Politics Beyond the Uprisings: Experiments in an Era of Resurgent Authoritarianism*, ed. Thanassis Cambanis and Michael Wahid Hanna (New York: Century Foundation Press, 2017), 73–101.

32. Victoria Yan, "'Business as Usual' for Gulf Lebanese," *Daily Star*, November 14, 2017; Associated Press, "Hariri Resignation Sends Lebanon's Economy back into Crisis," November 11, 2017; and Sami Aboudi, "Lebanese Expats Fearful as Gulf Expels Dozens Accused of Hezbollah Links," Reuters, April 8, 2016, http://www.reuters.com/article/us-gulf-hezbollah-lebanon/lebanese-expats-fearful-as-gulf-expels-dozens-accused-of-hezbollah-links-idUSKCN0X51R2.

33. Glen Carey, Vivian Nereim, and Christopher Cannon, "Sun, Sea and Robots: Saudi Arabia's Sci-Fi City in the Desert," Bloomberg, October 26, 2017, https://www.bloomberg.com/graphics/2017-neom-saudi-mega-city/.

34. Vivian Nereim and Alaa Shahine, "Saudi Arabia Crown Prince Details Plans for New City: Transcript," Bloomberg, October 26, 2017, https://www.bloomberg.com/news/articles/2017-10-26/saudi-arabia-crown-prince-details-plans-for-new-city-transcript.

35. Marc Lynch, *Voices of the New Arab Public: Iraq, Al-Jazeera, and Middle East Politics Today* (New York: Columbia University Press, 2007).

36. MBC Group, http://www.mbc.net/en/corporate.html; and Dubai Media City, http://www.dmc.ae/en/. On art city, see Louvre Museum, https://www.louvre.fr/en; and Art Dubai Fair, http://www.artdubai.ae/.

37. Alanoud Alsharekh and Robert Springborg, eds., *Popular Culture and Political Identity in the Arab Gulf States* (London: Saqi Books, 2008).

38. Ridab Nahar, "'Hams Al Hareer' Professes the Fixations of the Emirati Woman," Alarab, April 5, 2014, http://alarab.co.uk/?id=19402.

39. Al Itihad, "Emirates Youth Associations Launches 'Our Youth,'" January 28, 2018,

http://www.alittihad.ae/details.php?id=6499&y=2018.

40. Image Nation Abu Dhabi, "Hayati Walaskariya (My Life/My Military)," YouTube, 1:00, March 1, 2014, https://www.youtube.com/watch?v=8MDzorapvjo.

41. Zain, "Ramadan Zain 'Alan 2017,'" YouTube, 3:11, March 26, 2017, https://www.youtube.com/watch?v=U49nOBFv508.

42. Cairo Post, "Full Text of Sisi's Speech at New Suez Canal Inauguration Ceremony," August 6, 2015, http://thecairopost.youm7.com/news/163086/news/full-text-of-sisis-speech-at-new-suez-canal-inauguration-ceremony.

43. Sarah Carr, "President Sisi's Canal Extravaganza," *Foreign Policy*, August 7, 2015, http://foreignpolicy.com/2015/08/07/sisi-dredges-the-depth-egypt-suez-canal-boondoggle/.

44. Many renditions of the song can be found on YouTube. For example, see Ninette, "Teslam el Ayadi with English Captions," YouTube, August 4, 2013, https://www.youtube.com/watch?v=jDgyzOTmeiY.

45. Amr Adly, "The Problematic Continuity of Nasserism," Jaddaliya, March 31, 2014, http://www.jadaliyya.com/pages/index/17135/the-problematic-continuity-of-nasserism.

46. Al Ahram Weekly, http://weekly.ahram.org.eg/; Al Ahram Hebdo, http://hebdo.ahram.org.eg/; Al Shaab, http://www.elshaab.org/; Al-Gumhuriya, http://www.aljoumhouria.com/; and Akhbar Al-Adab, https://adab.akhbarelyom.com/.

47. Anouar Abdel-Malek, *Egypt: Military Society: The Army Regime, the Left, and Social Change Under Nasser* (New York: Random House, 1968).

48. Patrick Kingsley, "Egyptian TV Crew Criticized over Police Raid on Cairo Bath House," *Guardian*, December 9, 2014, https://www.theguardian.com/world/2014/dec/09/egypt-police-raid-cairo-bath-house.

49. Patrick Kingsley, "Egypt's Censorship of Comedian Bassem Youssef Sends 'Wrong Message,'" *Guardian*, January 25, 2014, https://www.theguardian.com/world/2014/jan/26/egypt-censorship-bassem-youssef-tv-satirist.

50. Sarah El Deeb, "British-Lebanese TV Host Deported from Egypt to Beirut," Associated Press, June 28, 2016, https://apnews.com/9b07d19a69be41428eb0725f42a278e9.

51. Dalia Said Mostafa, *The Egyptian Military in Popular Culture: Context and Critique* (Manchester, UK: Palgrave MacMillan, 2017), 124; and Amr Adly, "Egypt's Conservative Nationalism: Discourse and Praxis in the New Regime," Jadaliyya, October 14, 2014, http://www.jadaliyya.com/pages/index/19628/egypt%E2%80%99s-conservative-nationalism_discourse-and-pra. For more beyond the cultural field, see Amr Adly, "The Military Economy and the Future of the Private Sector in Egypt," Carnegie Middle East Center, September 6, 2014, http://carnegie-mec.org/2014/09/06/military-economy-and-future-of-private-sector-in-egypt-pub-56568; and Yezid Sayigh, "Above the State: The Officer's Republic in Egypt," Carnegie Middle East Center, August 1, 2012, http://carnegie-mec.org/2012/08/01/above-state-officers-republic-in-egypt-pub-48972.

4

Are Middle Eastern Militaries
Agents of Stability or Instability?

FLORENCE GAUB

Although the Arab Spring was hailed as the beginning of a new
political era in the region, it actually heralded the start of a decade
dominated by the military. What began with the armed forces of Tunisia
and Egypt facilitating regime change continued with military forces disin-
tegrating in Libya and Yemen, a full-blown civil war in Syria, a protracted
counterinsurgency in Iraq, and a war conducted by Saudi Arabia and the
United Arab Emirates (UAE) in Yemen. Even relatively stable forces in
countries such as Algeria, Jordan, Lebanon, and Morocco struggle with
the impact of regional spillover. Consequently, casualty rates have been
consistently high since 2011 with 30,000–50,000 a year killed across the
region, and defense spending has hovered between 5 and 6 percent of gross
domestic product (GDP) in many countries.[1]

Nonstate actors have eaten away at the military's (theoretical) monop-
oly on the use of force as they have grown in both strength and numbers.
More than 20 groups (half operating in Syria) now have guided light weapons such as man-portable air defense systems and anti-tank guided weapons. The Houthis in Yemen and the Islamic State in Iraq and Syria managed
to seize sovereign state territory, and new groups have emerged in Egypt
and Libya. Substantial nonstate actors now operate in nearly every country
in the region.[2]

While these recent developments have brought Arab military forces
back to the center of attention, this merely continues a trend present
since the era of independence: Military forces in the Middle East and
North Africa are more at the center of instability than being providers of
security. Since 1932, the year of Iraqi independence, they have interfered
in politics, attempting 73 coups across the region and succeeding in 39.

Over the same time frame, they have engaged in seven interstate wars, eight civil wars, and at least 10 counterinsurgency operations. Arab military forces have also performed poorly on the tactical level, leading in Iraq, Lebanon, Libya, and Yemen to the disintegration of the forces as a whole. The dysfunctional nature of Arab armies has had costly effects: at least 1.3 million people killed, more than $12 trillion spent, and many missed opportunities for political and economic integration of Arab states since the end of World War II.[3]

As decision makers inside and outside the region seek to improve the performance of Arab armed forces, they must consider why Arab militaries are so often destabilizing. There can be no solution without addressing the forces' endemic institutional weakness and the dysfunctional nature of civil-military relations in the region.

Elements of Institutional Weakness

Whether military forces in the Middle East and North Africa descend from colonial forces or tribal fighters, they share a number of institutional traits that ultimately lead to poor efficiency: They are underfunded, recruit poorly, lack transparency in the appointment and promotion of officers, demand only low education, and "cut and paste" doctrine rather than innovate.

No Money, No Military. The Middle East and North Africa have a history of proportionately high defense spending. Average military spending across the region now stands at 5–6 percent of GDP. In comparison, European states spend, on average, 1.3 percent. Military spending peaked in 1982, when Iraq spent 23.25 percent, Syria spent 17 percent, and both Saudi Arabia and Jordan spent 14 percent of their budgets on defense. On average, the region has consistently exceeded Western levels of defense spending since the 1970s.

Admittedly, such numbers do not always amount to much in absolute terms: In 1977, for instance, Iraq's 11.7 percent equaled only $1.6 billion, whereas the United States' 6.5 percent totaled $109.7 billion. Although high oil prices sometimes enabled greater spending in nominal terms, Middle Eastern armies generally operate with limited resources. This is particularly the case for non-oil-producing states: In 1973, Lebanon spent just $75 million, Jordan spent just $143 million, and Tunisia spent just $39 million.[4] Although regional GDP increased as a whole, Arab states still operate with only 20–25 percent of the total resources that American and European states have at their disposal.[5]

Resource restrictions have several implications. They slow down the acquisition of military equipment, hamper maintenance, hinder tactical performance, and lower morale. In addition, statistics show that the lower the spending on defense, the more likely a coup d'état becomes.[6]

Even where Arab forces had adequate equipment, poor maintenance was (and generally still is) a severe issue, leading to operational readiness rates ranging between 50 and 67 percent. In comparison, the US military averages a readiness rate of 90 percent.[7] In part, this is because Arab combat units lack personnel capable of making repairs and because soldiers and officers often lack the training and knowledge to exploit all their weapons' possibilities.[8] Lack of funds certainly played a role in the decisions of the Egyptian, Iraqi, Libyan, Sudanese, and Syrian officer corps to stage coups. In several instances, the plotters' first declaration included requests for increased spending.

While general frustration over low military spending may be institutional, it is also personal: The largest chunk of the defense budget in most Arab countries is spent on salaries rather than equipment. This in turn reverberates through society. In 2017, for every 1,000 Saudi citizens, 8.1 are in the military. The proportion is greater in Lebanon (10.34) and Jordan (12.25). In comparison, the United States' ratio stands at 4.1 and France's at 2.98. As a result, 75 percent of Lebanon's $1.74 billion defense budget covers wages—which are low compared to engineers, doctors, lawyers, or architects—placing officers in the middle- and lower-middle-class section of society. In Egypt, a colonel takes home $460 a month, and a major general $590, with their Algerian and Iraqi counterparts taking home only slightly more. Although officers in the Persian Gulf might make more than that—a colonel in the UAE military takes home $25,000 a month (a sixfold increase from 2008)—they are still in the midsection of their respective societies.[9]

Except for Lebanon and Mauritania, salaries have increased in all Arab forces since 2011, perhaps in recognition of the demoralizing effect of low salaries. Algerian military salaries increased 40 percent, while Qatar military salaries increased 120 percent. Pay also increased in Egypt, Morocco, Saudi Arabia, and Syria (although they remain below $100 a month).[10] While Iraqi soldiers received no salary increase, they were exempt from the cuts affecting other public-sector employees after 2014.

Some decision makers in the region have sought to work around budgetary constraints by allowing their armed forces to engage in economic activities. Among Arab states, the Egyptian military's enterprises are probably the most known in this regard, as they not only have expanded into clearly civilian industries such as the production of household items (e.g., air conditioners, baby formula, and refrigerators) but also make up an important yet unknown share of Egypt's economy (estimates range between 5 and 60 percent).[11] But Egypt is not the only case: Before the civil war, Syria's military was active in the civilian construction sector and produced non-military items such as food, furniture, and medicines. In Iraq, the military was involved in the production of electronics, plastics, and engines for the civilian market.

Arab militaries often turn blind eyes toward other mechanisms of their members' enrichment. The practice of "ghost soldiering," in which commanding officers pocket the salaries of real or fictitious absentees, became a growing problem in Iraq in the 1990s, when the government in Baghdad could not afford lavishing extras on officers as it had in the pre-sanctions era. Although not comparable, the involvement of many Persian Gulf officers in their own side businesses, such as travel agencies and import-export companies, also erodes military morale because it dilutes the sense of purpose and civic duty, making the military just a job among others. Taken together, the blurring of lines between military and business harms the civilian sector, invites corruption, and distracts from the military's core business, defense of the country.

Recruiting for Success? Of course, financial considerations are not the only ingredient in military performance; the officer corps is also important. Arab armed forces have continuously struggled with recruitment due to both selection methods and the poor quality of available candidates.[12]

Finding qualified young men and, in a few cases, women whom the military can tap has been difficult for several reasons. Until about 1990, the region suffered from high illiteracy and poor education. For instance, at the time of the 1967 war, fewer than 2 percent of Egyptian officers had a university degree, and the rank and file were largely illiterate; 50 years later they still are.

Since then, numerous reform programs have borne fruit. Literacy has improved dramatically. By 2010, 81 percent of Middle Eastern adults were literate, and that figure is even higher among 15- to 24-year-olds. In addition, the pool of individuals from whom to choose has grown several times over and, given demographic trends, will continue to do so. For example, Egypt had a population of 27 million in 1960 and has 93 million today; Jordan had 900,000 in 1960 and has eight million today. In theory, Arab forces therefore have a larger and better educated pool from which to choose than they had in the 1960s. This matters because, in the words of Nathan Toronto, a professor at the UAE National Defense College, an officer's education "provides an intellectual architecture for battlefield success. It contributes to stable civil-military relations, a culture of reflection, and a capacity for critical analysis."[13]

The size of the recruiting pool is only academic, however, unless individuals apply to the armed forces—and for the "right" reasons. In the West, this means a desire for camaraderie, enjoyment of physical activity, and an appreciation of nationalism. However, in the Middle East, the economy influences the motivation to join the armed forces, and, when the motive is primarily financial, it can hurt morale and performance.[14]

Unemployment among military-age males has hovered between 25 and 30 percent for decades, even in many of the oil-rich Persian Gulf states. Young unemployed men long figured that the military could offer employment and that a stable geostrategic environment meant that the chance of being involved in war was low. Hence, the armed forces became more of an occupation than a profession. As one recruit noted about his Egyptian superiors:

> It was different in the old days; back then they had a cause to fight for—now it's all just bullshit and corruption, just another job for most of the personnel. Most of the mid-ranking officers are completely uninterested in all the patriotic rhetoric. For them it's just stable employment with decent benefits.[15]

While Middle Eastern militaries can do little to change the educational levels and motivations of the candidates, they can improve both the process and the results.

Except for Algeria, most Arab militaries have not historically run recruitment campaigns to attract the most qualified and motivated candidates. For years, most would do what Saudi Arabia and Tunisia still do and simply publish a call for applications in the official news outlet. Iraqi military decision makers, for instance, believed that, so long as the number of applicants was high, they could not justify spending on more targeted recruitment. Lebanon's sectarian quotas only exacerbate this situation. Traditionally, the Lebanese Armed Forces attract a far lower number of Christian applicants to the officer corps than Muslim, but since parity in the corps is guaranteed, Muslim candidates face greater competition for officer slots than their Christian counterparts. The perception that Christians are "quota officers" can affect cohesion.

But there is growing recognition that this misreads quantity for quality. Jordan's King Abdullah II issued a directive in 2015 to "revisit the methodology of recruiting officers and trajectory of their military career with the aim of enhancing the capabilities of the armed forces and upgrading the skills of their members . . . [to] attract qualified young Jordanians and encourage them to join the ranks of the armed forces." As a result, Jordan launched a recruitment program seeking university graduates to join the officer corps.[16] In Lebanon, where the number of Christians applying for the ranks has dropped, commanding officers now can bypass formal recruitment procedures for Christians.

Recent crises have also caused governments to rethink recruitment policies. After Iraq's armed forces collapsed in 2014 in the face of the Islamic State, they suffered as an attractive employer and so launched a recruitment campaign including YouTube videos, a weekly national TV show, and a newspaper.[17] Unfortunately, the campaign did not fully succeed. Joining the paramilitary Popular Mobilization Units was more attractive to many young men because they are less strict in their training, rotations, and recruitment procedures and easier to join than the more professional military.

Lastly, Syria's armed forces, which have suffered desertion rates as high as 50 percent, have also launched a large recruitment campaign to increase manpower. It has offered prisoners amnesty in exchange for military service. And throughout the civil war, Syria has continued officer recruitment and education.[18] However, such a recruitment drive does not necessarily recruit the best possible candidates, especially when the Syrian leadership is loath to turn away candidates.

If recruitment is one strategy, compulsory military service is another. Algeria, Egypt, Sudan, Syria, and Tunisia have long used conscription. Both Kuwait and Yemen suspended conscription but then reinstated it. Qatar and the UAE introduced it for the first time in 2014. The non-Arab states Iran, Israel, and Turkey also conscript. While Iraq, Jordan, Lebanon, and Morocco have abolished (or "paused") conscription, Bahrain, Oman, and Saudi Arabia are the only Arab states that have never had conscription. Yet even in these countries, former military officers and even religious authorities often call to implement conscription.[19]

Conscription can serve different purposes. While it is a civic duty designed to instill national values and foster cohesion, it also has an operational purpose in countries such as Egypt and Syria, which have relied for long periods on the manpower-intensive Soviet doctrine. Both states have deployed conscripts into operational theatres. Egypt, for example, has sent conscripts into the Sinai Peninsula, while Syria has put them on the front lines of the civil war. Poorly equipped and trained, they suffer high casualties and low morale.[20] Low pay—just $35 a month in Egypt—does not improve matters.[21]

For those countries that conscript, it is difficult to dodge the draft. There are no legal provisions to object on the grounds of conscience, and often the only alternative is emigration. Recently, even though it put a hold on implementing the draft, Jordan has restricted travel for young men who have not registered with the military.[22]

While Middle Eastern militaries make little effort to attract the best officer candidates, they compensate with a strict selection process. In Egypt, for instance, the entry exam is open only to candidates possessing a general secondary school certificate showing above-average grades. The exam consists of a competitive academic examination, a medical examination, and a physical fitness test. With these measures in place, President Anwar Sadat increased the number of officers with a university degree from 2 to 60 percent within six years when barely 20 percent of Egypt's population could read and write.[23]

But these meritocratic principles are regularly undermined by the application of nonmilitary criteria across the region. These can be religious, ethnic, social, tribal, or regional. The problem with biased recruitment is twofold: On one hand, it undermines meritocratic principles and cohesion. On the other, it politicizes the officer corps as recruitment "stacks" certain groups of society against others. A transparent quota such as in Lebanon is less harmful to cohesion than a covert one, especially if the goal of biased recruitment is political stability rather than political control.

A counterexample is Iraq. Article IX of the constitution states: "The Iraqi armed forces and security services will be composed of the components of the Iraqi people with due consideration given to their balance and representation without discrimination or exclusion." The problem with this *implicit* quota is that it does not define "components"—which could be regional, religious, or ethnic—and it does not state how to measure "balance." The lack of reliable statistics on Iraq's different groups only compounds the problem. As a result, Article IX has served as a tool to cement Shi'a Arab dominance in the lower officer ranks based on the assumption that they make up 60 percent of Iraq's population. In contrast to Lebanon, Iraq's quota is neither transparent nor a signal of legal parity of Iraq's three ethnic or sectarian groups. The impact on Iraqi military cohesion has been severe.

Syria, too, used a covertly biased recruitment process to increase the share of the Alawi minority in the officer ranks of the armed forces. Although Alawis make up perhaps only 12 percent of the population, 61 percent of officers appointed between 1970 and 1997 were Alawi. While the regime sought to gloss over this by appointing Sunnis and Christians to visible posts, it nevertheless hurt Sunni officers' morale. Alawis were given preferential treatment in recruitment and promotion, thereby hindering Sunni career advancement.[24]

Biased recruitment in the Middle East and North Africa is not solely sectarian. In Jordan, the divide between urban and Bedouin populations has permeated the armed forces from their inception in 1920. Originally manned almost exclusively with tribal fighters, the armed forces had to take in educated urbanites once they began expansion into modern technology. The antagonism between the two groups nearly led to a coup in 1956; its failure ultimately strengthened the tribal claim to the armed forces.[25] So strong is the tribal component in the Jordanian military's image that the recruitment call for university graduates was accompanied by the message that "enrollment will be completely based on 'competency,' rather than any nepotistic connections," which led a news website to comment, "The issues in question, however, will be the impartiality of recruiting committees in establishing equal opportunities for all Jordanians alike—within a strong tribal current."[26]

Biased recruitment can be ideological as well. In Egypt, personnel with Islamist tendencies have come under severe scrutiny since the 1981 assassination of Sadat, if not before. This suspicion against Islamists has intensified since the 2013 coup, when the military removed Mohamed Morsi, the democratically elected president and a Muslim Brotherhood member. Recruits are being carefully screened by not only military intelligence but also staff within the ranks. "It is logical and normal that we monitor deviant thinking. Any armed forces must have loyalty and we take all the measures needed against others," one Egyptian officer explained. While the numbers of Islamists in the ranks might be low, it is not zero. A handful of officers have left the Egyptian military and joined the Islamist insurgency in the Sinai Peninsula since the coup, and military sources confirm that "there are individual members of the army who we discover possess extremist religious thoughts. But their numbers are very few. Maybe two or three in a class of 2,000."[27]

The exclusion of elements with subversive tendencies is certainly not unique to the Egyptian military. For example, before Recep Tayyip Erdoğan's rise to power in Turkey, the Turkish military acted as the guardians of secularism and purged officers deemed Islamist. In Egypt, however, military screening mirrors the larger political struggle in which the borders among religiosity, political activism, and radicalism are blurred.

Training, Education, and Strategic Thinking. While the pool of military personnel might be flawed and recruitment methods could be improved, Middle Eastern militaries struggle with education and training. Education and training not only transmit military know-how such as the handling of weapons but also build cohesion, discipline, and combat readiness. When flawed, they undermine strategic thinking. Levels of education and training vary across the region but never approach the level of Western military forces. However, the strategic instability following the events of 2011 has given new impulse to these areas, leading to potential improvements.

In Egypt, for instance, the military has institutionalized officer education since the 1960s, when it founded the Nasser High Military Academy. In addition, the Egyptian military has often sent officers abroad to the United States and Europe. Strategic exercises take place regularly. In 2016 alone, Egypt conducted 30 joint military exercises with countries in the region and with Europe and the United States, the largest one being the Aqaba exercise with Jordan. The problems lie more at the tactical level, which the Egyptian military has neglected since updating training in the 1970s.[28] This became evident during the 2011 protest when soldiers handled tanks and armored personnel carriers poorly, accidentally injuring protesters.

In Iraq, both training and education encountered severe difficulties in the post-invasion environment. Preinvasion US plans foresaw a recall of the armed forces (almost half a million troops at the time), but the Coalition Provisional Authority (CPA) under L. Paul Bremer disbanded it, although recall programs were already operating.[29] Compounding the problem was that, despite Bremer's statements to the contrary, the army's disbandment was not followed by a thorough plan to create "an entirely new Iraqi army."[30] The small force of 44,000, focused entirely on external security without an air force, tank, or artillery corps, took a remarkably long time to build. Almost a year after the invasion, barely 10,000 troops had been recalled to duty although Iraq's security was imploding.

When the file was moved from the CPA to the American military, recruitment and recall programs increased almost eightfold within a year. Military planners abandoned plans for a small force. Every five weeks, 14,000 men integrated into the new Iraqi army. By 2005, the force's size was 130,000; by 2008, it had grown to 200,000 (180,000 enlisted personnel and 20,000 officers), and the reconstituted military also changed its focus to counterterrorism and counterinsurgency. Within six years, the Iraqi military quadrupled in size.

But there are several problems with any force growing this quickly. While almost all troops received basic training, its length and content varied greatly.[31] Returnees of the old Iraqi army, for instance, received three weeks of training, whereas newcomers underwent between five and 13 weeks; in some instances, training from the Saddam-era was counted.[32]

Training alone does not make an armed force, especially one built from scratch. It is usually most effective in units with existing structures, experienced officers, noncommissioned officers, and teams. The rushed creation of whole new units is always difficult, and it requires time and, most importantly, officers. The Iraqi military lacked (and still lacks) officers, who in turn need time and training to grow. As Gen. Martin Dempsey stated in 2007:

> We've been growing young second lieutenants through the military academies for about three years, but it's really difficult to grow majors, lieutenant colonels, and brigadier generals. It simply can't be done overnight. So we've had to rely heavily on officer recalls and retraining programs. However, the pool of qualified recalls is beginning to thin out.[33]

Education was slow to take off, particularly for officers. The military academy in Ar-Rustamiyah, where basic officer training takes places, was reopened only in 2007, and the Iraqi War College, which offers education for officers up to the rank of colonel, was opened in 2010. Once left in the hands of Prime Minister Nouri al-Maliki, Iraq's military became more politicized: The prime minister's office allotted education spots, and training below battalion level became rare for fear of a coup. By 2014, when crucial Iraqi army units collapsed in the face of the Islamic State, Dempsey, then the chairman of the Joint Chiefs of Staff, stated that only around half of Iraqi combat brigades could be deemed "reputable partners."[34] American support has since focused on correcting these wrongs: Over three years, more than 35,000 troops were trained, but the main issue remains the officer corps, which is understaffed and politicized and struggles with strategic thinking.

In Tunisia, the absence of significant threats until 2011 left the armed forces with training schedules and programs entirely unsuited for terrorism, which manifested itself after the Arab Spring and the collapse of Libya. Neither Saudi Arabia nor the UAE took training seriously until recently. Involvement in the Yemen conflict has triggered a change in this thinking.

The absence of stringent education and training programs is mirrored in the poor strategic thinking in most military decision-making circles. Most Arab states—including Algeria, Egypt, Tunisia, and Yemen—have no national security strategy. Iraq and Lebanon developed their plans only after major internal conflicts. Several states confuse strategy with doctrine. Doctrine defines a standard set of maneuvers, troops, and weapons that are employed as a default approach to an attack. Strategy, in contrast, defines an overarching plan to achieve one or more goals under conditions of uncertainty. This, however, remains entirely in the realm of civilian decision-making in most Arab states.

Civil-Military Relations in the Middle East and North Africa

There is little study on the interaction between civilian and military decision makers in the region largely because most research focuses on the relations between democratically elected civilians and their military counterparts, but most civilians in the Middle East do not operate in democratic environments. Regardless of how they came to power, civilians do play a crucial role in shaping the military's role, performance, and image.

Civil-military relations are often reduced to civilian oversight or control of the armed forces because of the asymmetric nature of the relationship: The military can, at least in theory, violently overthrow the government. Depending on context, it takes as little as 2 percent of an armed force to stage a coup against a regime, with critical units being as small as a battalion (about 1,000 troops) and the number of officers ranging somewhere between 30 and 50.

While this asymmetry overshadows the relationship, the interaction is nevertheless more complex. In strategic and operational matters, civilian leaders must rely on military expertise to make their decisions. Similarly, for the relations to be as productive as possible, agreement on key points—such as the composition of the officer corps, the decision-making process, recruitment methods, and doctrine—is desirable.[35] But for relations to be constructive, each side requires certain characteristics: A military institution with coherence, autonomy, an identity, and a clear vision of its role will be able to provide useful insight, whereas civilians have more influence if they have legitimacy, institutions to exert their oversight, and trust in their armed forces.

By and large, civilian leaders in the Middle East have struggled with these attributes—in part, because their legitimacy was doubtful at times. Understanding in this context the different types of legitimacy is important: While Western systems provide *legal* legitimacy, charismatic legitimacy is derived from an individual's personality valued by the population, and traditional legitimacy is based on an inherited, established, or customary system over time. While certain Middle Eastern leaders have managed to rely, at least briefly, on charismatic and traditional legitimacy, the vast majority have had to make up for a legitimacy deficit not only in the eyes of the public but also in their relations with the armed forces.

The other component that makes civilians stronger in their interaction with the military is trust. Middle Eastern leaders, whether they reached power with the armed forces' help or not, face an implicit risk of removal by their armed forces, as every single Arab country and Turkey have seen at least one attempt since 1945. For all these reasons, Middle Eastern civilians have taken destructive measures to strengthen their position in civil-military relations.[36]

Lastly, a third component of civil-military relations is civil society in general, as it can act as a referee in the power struggle between armed forces and civilian leaders. Large-scale demonstrations against or for a coup can propel or stop a military force from intervening. In countries such as Jordan, Lebanon, and Tunisia, where the political culture is not permissive of a coup, civil society restricts the room for maneuvering against civilians.

Meddling with Military Mechanisms for Political Purposes. Civilians in the Middle East have weakened their armed forces in a number of ways.[37] For instance, they have exploited ethnic and religious identities for staffing purposes, usually supported by minorities who dominate officer slots, since they have incentive to maintain the status quo.[38] But even this is not enough to guarantee regime survival. Coups against co-ethnic or coreligionist leaders have taken place in most countries: In Syria, Hafez al-Assad overthrew fellow Alawi Salah Jadid, and in Iraq, the coups of 1958, 1963, and 1968 overthrew fellow Sunni Arabs. At least one coup attempt against Libyan leader Muammar Qadhafi, in 1993, was staged by officers from a tribe nominally loyal to him. In fact, most coups are staged from within the same ethnic or religious group precisely because grievances have accumulated in other overlooked dimensions of identity, such as ideology or professionalism.

Allowing the armed forces or its members to engage in economic activities that have no strict military purpose has the same purpose, as civilians hope to tie these benefits to their regime and thereby buy loyalty. But civilian leaders employing these strategies have not just unintentionally hurt cohesion; they have also undermined it to protect themselves from ouster. Civilians have therefore regularly chosen to hollow out cohesion at the expense of combat capacity. They have achieved this by frequently rotating officers to discourage strong ties, restricting training above certain unit levels, restricting access to ammunition, and centralizing soldiers' benefits such as pay to undermine the relationship with superior officers. Iraq, Libya, and to some extent Syria excelled at this practice, but traces of "coup-proofing" measures can be found in all military institutions across the region.

Civilian Supervision: The Unexplored Options. While civilians have the task of supervising and controlling Arab military forces, many civilian leaders cannot or do not fully supervise or control their militaries. In Egypt, for instance, the military's persistent influence in the halls of power has gradually eroded civilian supervision. Whereas the 1923 constitution declared the king to be the commander in chief, the subsequent Egyptian constitutions of 1971, 2012, and 2014 successively expanded the armed forces' power over their own affairs. The 2014 constitution went the furthest by declaring the defense minister to be the commander in chief (who, constitutionally, is always a military officer). The budget of the armed forces is not itemized, effectively eviscerating parliament's supervisory powers.

A different case is post-Saddam Iraq, where the legal framework for civil-military relations is sound in theory, but not in practice. Parliament takes a central stage in Iraqi defense matters, leaving the entire system lopsided when the parliament failed to exercise its supervision—in part due to the high levels of violence that made traveling to and from the Green Zone dangerous because boycotting the sessions had become a popular tool to express discontent and because it took nearly a year after the 2010 elections to form the government. Several times, sessions were adjourned because parliament could not achieve a quorum. In essence, this left the executive unchecked in defense matters and gave Maliki the opportunity to appoint and promote officers without parliamentary approval and to fire civilians from the defense ministry and replace them with military personnel. Prime Minister Haider Abadi's reforms since then have aimed at reestablishing Iraq's balance of civil-military relations, including a reform of the defense ministry and regular testimony to parliament's defense committee.

The Iraqi case underlines the fact that, while parliaments play a crucial role in Western civil-military relations, they generally fail to do the same in the Middle East. There are three reasons for this: Where parliaments have been elected democratically (Iraq, Lebanon, and Tunisia), they lack power over the executive's decisions as a result of immature civil-military relations, expertise, or collaborative spirit. Where parliaments have been elected in an authoritarian environment merely to validate the executive's decisions (Algeria, Egypt, and Morocco), they will not seek to exert civilian control. Lastly, in certain states (Bahrain aand Saudi Arabia) parliaments have been introduced comparatively recently and either are not entirely elected or have negligible decision-making power.

Similarly, ministries of defense, which can play a crucial role in formulating and implementing defense policies, play less of a supervisory role in the region than they could. Ministries are generally staffed with military rather than civilian staff, and the minister is often an officer, too. In Algeria, all 24 cabinets since 1962 have had a military defense minister, just as all 19 Egyptian defense ministers since 1952 have been from the military. This reduces civilian input even further. In addition, policymaking usually takes place at a higher strategic level, reducing the ministries to mere executors rather than shapers.

Effectively, the link between civilians and military in the Middle East is weak and permeated by distrust rather than by the desire to jointly form strategic decisions. Consequently, the number of cases in which Arab civilians ignored military input on defense matters is high and came generally at a high strategic cost: This has been true with King Farouk and Morsi in Egypt and was true for Saddam Hussein during the Iran-Iraq War. It is also true for one-time military leaders who essentially "civilianize" themselves with time, such as Qadhafi, who ignored military advice during the war with Chad. In such cases, civil society cannot provide a check. In most countries, civil society plays no role beyond publicly acclaiming the armed forces, and in some states such as Egypt, publicly criticizing or questioning the armed forces is even illegal, stifling debate even further.

Ultimately, all these developments have led to the fragmentation of Middle Eastern security sectors. Because Arab civilians distrusted their armed forces politically, they have encouraged or tolerated the creation of paramilitary actors, such as armed wings of political parties (such as Hezbollah in Lebanon), militias (such as in Iraq or Libya), and fulfill military tasks. And they have created security agencies to monitor armed forces. The emergence of actors such as the Islamic State merely continues a phenomenon that ultimately expresses state weakness in defense matters.

Nevertheless, these forces are unlikely to replace conventional military force in the near future. Without technology, heavy artillery, intelligence, and air or naval power, militias cannot conduct full-blown war. However, militias can supplement conventional forces: They act exclusively as infantry units, deploy rapidly because their command structure is less cumbersome, and display generally high levels of morale because they are often ideologically motivated. But herein lies also their limit: Militias are rarely seen as agents of the nation, but rather as expressions of particular interests. While their morale might be high, training levels are low, and while they can act faster, they are also more likely to abuse their powers due to lack of supervision. Hence, militias are less likely to enjoy broad approval of the societies in which they operate.

This stands in contrast to conventional military forces, which enjoy rather positive images across the region. According to one survey conducted in Egypt, Iraq, Jordan, Lebanon, Mauritania, Saudi Arabia, Tunisia, and Yemen, 77 percent of citizens expressed a great deal or some trust in the armed forces.[39] Numbers were lower in Iraq and Yemen, but elsewhere a near consensus existed among Arab citizens.

Conclusion

For Arab military forces to improve their performance and capacity, crucial changes need to occur—in the forces themselves and in the way civilians interact with them. To some observers, such as Col. Norvell B. De Atkine, who served as a trainer for Arab militaries for several decades, culture is the main obstacle to qualitative change.[40] But this is somewhat simplistic: First, Russian forces display similar attributes but are still effective when fighting an insurgency, whether in Chechnya or Syria. Secondly, military transformation can occur against the backdrop of crisis. In fact, profound changes in human behavior are often the result of crisis.

This is already visible in some of the region's forces: The militaries in the Persian Gulf embarked on a transformation around the time of the invasion of Iraq, preparing them to seize the moment of the strategic vacuum in 2011 and shape the region politically and militarily. Saudi Arabia, previously a sleeping military giant, has been militarily involved in Yemen and has even envisaged sending troops to Syria. A good example for military transformation is the Lebanese military, which has undergone extensive changes since the Syrian withdrawal in 2005. It has moved with mixed results to secure large parts of the previously unsecured border and took the lead in expelling the Islamic State from Arsal, even as Hezbollah claimed the credit. One counterexample is Egypt, where a largely conventional force has been unable to end a low-scale insurgency in the Sinai Peninsula—largely because its approach remains conventional.

These small seeds of change will bear fruit only if military and civilian decision makers in the region understand the costly implications of the status quo and create environments where military forces have the necessary resources, strategic thinking, and staff to fully implement these changes.

Notes

1. International Institute for Strategic Studies, *The Military Balance 2017*, February 2017, 358–59, https://www.iiss.org/publications/the-military-balance/the-military-balance-2017.

2. International Institute for Strategic Studies, *The Military Balance 2017*, 309.

3. Sundeep Waslekar and Ilmas Futehally, *Cost of Conflict in the Middle East* (Mumbai, India: Strategic Foresight Group, 2009); and Florence Gaub, "Arab Wars: Calculating the Costs," EU Institute for Security Studies, October 4, 2017, https://www.iss.europa.eu/content/arab-wars-calculating-costs.

4. US Arms Control and Disarmament Agency, *World Military Expenditures and Arms Transfers 1966–1975,* 1976, 35–37.

5. Şevket Pamuk, "Estimating Economic Growth in the Middle East Since 1820," *Journal of Economic History* 66, no. 3 (September 2006): 809–28.

6. Gabriel Leon, "Loyalty for Sale? Military Spending and Coups d'Etat," *Public Choice* 159, nos. 3–4 (June 2014): 363–83; and Vincenzo Bove and Roberto Nisticò, "Coups d'Etat and Defense Spending: A Counterfactual Analysis," Public Choice 161, nos. 3–4 (December 2014): 321–44.

7. Michael E. O'Hanlon, "Is the Pentagon Headed for a Military Readiness Crisis?," *National Interest*, October 12, 2017, www.nationalinterest.org/feature/the-pentagon-headed-military-readiness-crisis-22645; and David Petraeus and Michael E. O'Hanlon, "The Myth of a U.S. Military 'Readiness' Crisis," *Wall Street Journal*, August 9, 2016, https://www.wsj.com/articles/the-myth-of-a-u-s-military-readiness-crisis-1470783221.

8. Kenneth M. Pollack, *Arabs at War: Military Effectiveness, 1948–1991* (Lincoln, NE: University of Nebraska Press, 2004), 567.

9. Kareem Shaheen, "Army and Police Officers' Dh100,000 Pension Gap," *National* (Abu Dhabi, United Arab Emirates), September 21, 2010, http://www.thenational.ae/news/uae-news/army-and-police-officers-dh100-000-pension-gap.

10. Jihad Yazigi, "Syria's War Economy," European Council on Foreign Relations, April 2014, 3, https://www.ecfr.eu/page/-/ECFR97_SYRIA_BRIEF_AW.pdf; Aujourd'hui le Maroc, "Budget 2013 du ministère de la défense: Hausse des salaires des militaires à partir de décembre," December 27, 2012, http://aujourdhui.ma/actualite/budget-2013-du-ministere-de-la-defense-hausse-des-salaires-des-militaires-a-partir-de-decembre-99537; and *Jordan Times*, "Army Personnel to Receive Salary Bonus," December 29, 2016, http://www.jordantimes.com/news/local/army-personnel-receive-salary-bonus.

11. Emily Crane Linn, "The Army and Its President," *Foreign Policy*, January 28, 2016, http://foreignpolicy.com/2016/01/28/the-army-and-its-president-egypt-sisi/.

12. NATO Research and Technology Organisation, *Recruiting and Retention of Military Personnel*, October 2007, http://www.nato.int/issues/women_nato/Recruiting%20&%20Retention%20of%20Mil%20Personnel.pdf.

13. Nathan W. Toronto, "Does Military Education Matter?," E-International Relations, May 26, 2015, http://www.e-ir.info/2015/05/26/does-military-education-matter/.

14. Jerald G. Bachman, Lee Sigelman, and Greg Diamond, "Self-Selection, Socialization, and Distinctive Military Values: Attitudes of High School Seniors," *Armed Forces*

and Society 13, no. 2 (Winter 1987): 169–87, https://deepblue.lib.umich.edu/handle/2027.42/68068.

15. Jack Shenker, "Egyptian Army Officer's Diary of Military Life in a Revolution," *Guardian*, December 28, 2011, https://www.theguardian.com/world/2011/dec/28/egyptian-military-officers-diary.

16. *Jordan Times*, "Army Directed to Revisit Officers' Recruitment, Career Path Policies," June 1, 2015, http://jordantimes.com/news/local/army-directed-revisit-officers%E2%80%99-recruitment-career-path-policies; NOW, "Jordan Army Launches Recruitment Drive," July 7, 2014, https://now.mmedia.me/lb/en/archive/554873-jordan-army-launches-recruitment-drive (unavailable June 14, 2019); and Dala Jebril-Rogers, "Graduate 'Knights of the Future' Recruited in Jordan," *New Arab*, June 3, 2015, https://www.alaraby.co.uk/english/features/2015/6/3/graduate-knights-of-the-future-recruited-in-jordan.

17. Renad Mansour, "Your Country Needs You: Iraq's Faltering Military Recruitment Campaign," Carnegie Middle East Center, July 22, 2015, http://carnegie-mec.org/diwan/60810.

18. Kheder Khaddour, "Strength in Weakness: The Syrian Army's Accidental Resilience," Carnegie Middle East Center, March 14, 2016, http://carnegie-mec.org/2016/03/14/strength-in-weakness-syrian-army-s-accidental-resilience-pub-62968.

19. BBC Monitoring International Reports, "Saudi Mufti Urges Compulsory Military Service of Youths–Pan-Arab Daily Report," *Al-Quds al-Arabi*, April 11, 2015; BBC Monitoring International Reports, "Saudi Paper Highlights Benefits of Military Conscription, Urges State to Recruit," Al-Watan, February 11, 2016; and Elizabeth Picard, "Arab Military in Politics: From Revolutionary Plot to Authoritarian Regime," in *The Arab State*, ed. Giacomo Luciani (London: Routledge, 1990), 202–8.

20. Louisa Loveluck, "New Recruitment Drive Indicates Deep Manpower Problems in Syria's Army," *Washington Post*, November 22, 2016, https://www.washingtonpost.com/world/middle_east/syrian-army-announces-new-volunteer-force-to-fight-terrorism/2016/11/22/d7a8aea2-b0bd-11e6-bc2d-19b3d759cfe7_story.html; Al-Masdar News, "Syria: Conscripts from Aleppo Join Syrian Army Ranks," July 1, 2017, https://www.almasdarnews.com/article/syria-conscripts-aleppo-join-syrian-army-ranks/; and Agence France-Presse, "With Aleppo Advance, Syria Army Sweeps Up Conscripts," *Daily Mail*, December 15, 2016, http://www.dailymail.co.uk/wires/afp/article-4035978/With-Aleppo-advance-Syria-army-sweeps-conscripts.html.

21. Middle East Eye, "'It Is Hell': Chronicles of Military Conscripts in Egypt," October 21, 2016, http://www.middleeasteye.net/in-depth/features/it-hell-chronicles-military-conscripts-egypt-army-university-1506222876; and Emir Nader, "Egypt's Draft Dodgers," Al-Monitor, July 22, 2015, http://www.al-monitor.com/pulse/originals/2015/07/egypt-military-conscription-sinai-attacks.html.

22. *Financial Times*, "Jordan Restricts Travel by Men of Military Age," June 26, 2014, https://www.ft.com/content/2059c816-fd51-11e3-96a9-00144feab7de.

23. Joseph Kechichian and Jeanne Nazimek, "Challenges to the Military in Egypt," *Middle East Policy Council* 5, no. 3 (Fall 1997), http://www.mepc.org/challenges-military-egypt; Arne Hoel, "Education in the Middle East and North Africa," World Bank, January 27, 2014, http://www.worldbank.org/en/region/mena/brief/education-in-mena;

and Yezid Sayigh, *Above the State: The Officers' Republic in Egypt*, Carnegie Middle East Center, August 1, 2012, http://carnegie-mec.org/2012/08/01/above-state-officers-republic-in-egypt-pub-48972.

24. Hicham Bou Nassif, "'Second-Class': The Grievances of Sunni Officers in the Syrian Armed Forces," *Journal of Strategic Studies* 38, no. 5 (2015): 626–49.

25. International Business Publications, *Jordan Country Study Guide, vol. 1, Strategic Information and Developments* (Alexandria, VA: International Business Publications, 2013), 79.

26. Jebril-Rogers, "Graduate 'Knights of the Future' Recruited in Jordan."

27. Yara Bayoumy, "In Egypt, Ex-Military Men Fire Up Islamist Insurgency," Reuters, April 7, 2015, http://uk.reuters.com/article/uk-egypt-militants-military-insight-idUKKBN0MY1PP20150407; and Ahmed Fouad, "Egypt May Ban Brotherhood Supporters from Joining Army," Al-Monitor, August 12, 2014, http://www.al-monitor.com/pulse/originals/2014/08/egypt-ban-recruitment-muslim-brotherhood-army.html.

28. Pollack, *Arabs at War*; and Marwa Awad, "Special Report: In Egypt's Military, a March for Change," Reuters, April 10, 2012, http://www.reuters.com/article/us-egypt-army-idUSBRE8390IV20120410.

29. James Pfiffner, "US Blunders in Iraq: De-Baathification and Disbanding the Army," *Intelligence and National Security* 25, no. 1 (February 2010): 76–85.

30. Douglas J. Feith, *War and Decision: Inside the Pentagon at the Dawn of the War on Terrorism* (New York: Harper, 2008), 432.

31. Anthony Cordesman, "The U.S. Transition in Iraq: Iraqi Forces and U.S. Military Aid," Center for Strategic and International Studies, October 21, 2010, 22, https://www.csis.org/analysis/us-transition-iraq-iraqi-forces-and-us-military-aid; Special Inspector General for Iraq Reconstruction, *Quarterly Report to the United States Congress*, July 30, 2010, 61; Special Inspector General for Iraq Reconstruction, *Quarterly Report to the United States Congress*, April 30, 2008, 98; and Anthony Cordesman, "Inexcusable Failure: Progress in Training the Iraqi Army and Security Forces as of Mid-July 2004," Center for Strategic and International Studies, July 20, 2004, 8, https://www.csis.org/analysis/inexcusable-failure-progress-training-iraqi-army-and-security-forces-mid-july-2004.

32. Carl D. Grunow, "Advising Iraqis: Building the Iraqi Army," *Military Review* (July–August 2006): 15, https://www.armyupress.army.mil/Journals/Military-Review/English-Edition-Archives/2006-Archive/.

33. Martin F. Dempsey, testimony before Subcommittee on Oversight and Investigations, Committee on Armed Services, US House of Representatives, June 12, 2007, https://www.govinfo.gov/content/pkg/CHRG-110hhrg38265/html/CHRG-110hhrg38265.htm.

34. Kirk Semple, "Iraq Army Woos Deserters Back to War on ISIS," *New York Times*, September 28, 2014, https://www.nytimes.com/2014/09/29/world/middleeast/iraq-army-woos-deserters-back-to-war-on-isis.html.

35. Rebecca L. Schiff, *The Military and Domestic Politics: A Concordance Theory of Civil-Military Relations* (New York: Routledge, 2009), 32–48.

36. Claude E. Welch and Arthur K. Smith, *Military Role and Rule: Perspectives on Civil-Military Relations* (Belmont, CA: Duxbury Press, 1974), 40.

37. James T. Quinlivan, "Coup-Proofing: Its Practice and Consequences in the

Middle East," *International Security* 24, no. 2 (Fall 1999): 133.

38. Nassif, "Second-Class"; Cynthia H. Enloe, *Ethnic Soldiers, State Security in Divided Societies* (Athens, GA: University of Georgia Press, 1980); Donald Horowitz, *Ethnic Groups in Conflict* (Berkeley, CA: University of California Press, 1985); and Theodore McLauchlin, "Loyalty Strategy and Military Defection in Rebellion," *Comparative Politics* 42, no. 3 (April 2010).

39. Arab Center for Research and Policy Studies, "The Arab Opinion Project: The Arab Opinion Index," March 2012, 47–48.

40. Norvell B. De Atkine, "Why Arabs Lose Wars," *Middle East Quarterly* 6, no. 4 (December 1999), http://www.meforum.org/441/why-arabs-lose-wars.

5

What Impact Does Education Have on Concepts of Citizenship?

MICHAEL A. FAHY

There was something palpably familiar about the background story of Mohamed Bouazizi, the 26-year-old Tunisian vegetable vender who, humiliated and despondent following serial confiscations of his wares by the police, set himself on fire—the proverbial spark that ignited what would become known as the Arab Spring. Reading the first reports of the incident, I had the sense that I had met this man—not in Tunisia in December 2010, but some 17 years earlier in Morocco.

The Moroccan man was a graduate of Mohammed V University with a degree in sociology. Like Bouazizi, he was a *chômeur diplomé* (holding a diploma with nowhere to go), tending a vegetable stand next to the central train station in Rabat and, on the occasion I met him, attempting for whatever reason to explain French philosopher Pierre Bourdieu's concept of social capital to an uncomprehending customer. Although it turned out that Bouazizi's university degree was apocryphal, the mythology surrounding him struck a powerful and relatable chord across the Arab world.

Bouazizi's story resonates with many young university graduates in the region. In September 2015, in one protest in front of the Egyptian Ministry of Higher Education, university students, frustrated by their inability to find work suitable to their advanced degrees, set fire to their PhD and MBA certificates.[1] The following year, a handful of members of the Moroccan "unemployed graduates" movement took the more drastic step of setting fire to themselves.[2]

It is impossible to get far in the literature—scholarly or otherwise—before encountering the word "crisis." "The [education] issue may not be in the daily headlines," the *Arab Weekly* wrote, "but is, in fact, one of the Arab world's biggest crises."[3] Coupling the terms "education" and "crisis" is not peculiar to the Arab world, nor is the narrative of the redemptive and transformative power of education. In May 2017, *New York Times* columnist David Leonhardt captured this notion when he wrote:

> Education isn't just another issue. It is the most powerful force for accelerating economic growth, reducing poverty and lifting middle-class living standards. Well-educated adults earn much more, live longer and are happier than poorly educated adults. When researchers try to tease out whether education does much to cause these benefits, the answer appears to be yes.[4]

The status of education as a force for personal advancement and social transformation remains a powerful narrative across the Arab world, but, in many instances, that status is equivocal.

Does Education Equal Opportunity?

There were approximately 100,000 university students in Morocco in the 1980s—a number that grew to more than a quarter million in the next decade. By the 2009–10 academic year, university enrollment in Morocco exceeded 308,000, with an additional 310,000 enrolled in vocational institutes.[5] That might seem positive, but enrollment does not equal prospects. In a country where the unemployment rate for the second quarter of 2017 was 9.3 percent, the highest unemployment rates were among 15- to 24-year-olds (23 percent), and those *with a diploma* clocked in at 17 percent.[6] Nor is this situation unique to Morocco.

Across the Middle East and North Africa (MENA), university enrollment has more than tripled since 1998 to close to 10 million today, and the sheer number of universities in the region more than doubled between 2003 and 2012 with close to 500 universities, a number increasing every year.[7] But simply building universities does not equate to meaningful employment for their graduates. In contrast to most developed and developing regions, data indicate that the unemployment rate among youth in the MENA region *increases* consistently with the level of education. Those with tertiary education are three times more likely to be unemployed than those with only a secondary degree or lower.[8] In Egypt and Tunisia, youth who complete their tertiary education are twice as likely to be unemployed as those with primary education or less.[9] The World Bank noted university graduates make up 30 percent of the region's unemployed.[10]

Part of the problem seems to be that population has outpaced university building. Not surprisingly, then, the preeminent issue engaging education researchers and analysts is not education per se, but rather how the demographic boom affects the education system. In 2016, the *Economist* noted that, since 1980, the Arab world's population has doubled to 357 million and may see another 110 million people added by 2025, almost twice the average global growth rate. The proportion of young people age 15–24 peaked in 2010 at 20 percent of the total population, but the absolute number of young people will keep growing from 46 million in 2010 to perhaps 58 million in 2025.[11]

This so-called youth bulge puts tremendous stress on educational infrastructures that have struggled to keep pace with expanding enrollments. The result has been educational systems that are overcrowded and overextended and a concomitant decline in the quality of schools as measured in terms of teacher-to-student ratios, resourcing and materials, testing performances, and limited or no access to technology that has become standard elsewhere for 21st-century classrooms.

In most of the Arab world, the upward mobility that education promised is lacking. There remains a stark lack of fit between the graduates educational institutions produce and the workforce countries need. Yet, across the region, many continue to embrace education as a means to accelerate economic growth and reduce poverty. Indeed, the day before the dramatic protests of university graduates burning their diplomas, the Egyptian Ministry of Higher Education was the site of protests by high school students and their parents demanding an *increase* in the admissions capacity of public universities. Such contradictions serve to underscore a profound tension between harnessing the seemingly transformative power of education and enduring frustration in the face of many obstacles.

Universities are, of course, only part of the educational landscape. At the primary and secondary levels of education, the Arab world has seen remarkable progress over the past few decades, during which most governments adopted vigorous state-mandated programs that included the development and expansion of enrollment and school infrastructure. At the primary level, the gross enrollment ratio rose from an average of 23.6 percent in 1950 to 75.6 percent in 1965 and 97.0 percent in 2000. The corresponding figures for secondary education are 3.8 percent in 1950, 22.6 percent in 1965, and 69.1 percent in 2000. By 2012, primary school enrollment rates exceeded 90 percent in a number of regional countries, including Algeria, Bahrain, Egypt, Jordan, Morocco, Qatar, Saudi Arabia, and the United Arab Emirates, on par with the world average. Access to education may not be completely uniform, but disparities are narrowing as Arab countries with low participation rates improve.[12]

Secondary school enrollment has improved as well, although dropout rates at the lower secondary school level have increased. While extending access to education is a considerable achievement, it is not enough. The challenges facing education systems and the societies they serve are formidable. And the closer the level of education is to preparation for and entry into the workforce, the more crisis-laden the discourse concerning education becomes.

Why Does Education Fall Short?

This crisis of education in the Arab world and its prospects for the future have been the focus of rigorous empirical studies and reports in recent years. Prominent among these have been the *Arab Human Development Reports* first issued under the auspices of the United Nations Development Programme (UNDP). The first report, released in 2002, critically evaluated the demographic, social, economic, and political conditions in the Arab region, provoking much soul-searching.[13] In the sixth and latest report, issued in 2016, many of the problems identified in 2002 remain unresolved.[14]

In 2014, the UNDP and Mohammed bin Rashid Al Maktoum Foundation published the extensive *Arab Knowledge Report 2014: Youth and Localisation of Knowledge*, which addresses the central role of knowledge production, transfer, and localization processes as the engine for human development. It also addresses the challenge of integrating youth in such processes in a region where they are largely marginalized and excluded.[15] After a May 2014

Global Education for All (GEA) meeting, UNESCO published "Regional Overview: Arab States,"[16] which assessed progress on the goals and strategies of UNESCO's GEA movement, "a global commitment to provide quality basic education for all children, youth and adults."[17]

Several think tanks and policy institutions have also examined education in the MENA region. One example includes the Brookings Institution's "The Paradox of Higher Education in MENA."[18] Increasingly, specialty blogs such as Al Fanar Media and Higher Education in the Arab Region also cover developments in Middle Eastern education policy and prospects.

There are considerable disparities among and within the countries that constitute the Arab region. All is not equal among the oil-rich Gulf Cooperation Council (GCC) states. Education in war-torn Syria and Yemen is in dire shape, and spillover has strained systems in Jordan and Lebanon. That said, there is nevertheless a consensus among the various studies on two points: First, the quality of higher education in the Arab region is among the lowest in the world, resulting in graduates being poorly prepared to meet the demands of the global marketplace. Second, genuine educational reform cannot be achieved without addressing the long-standing sociopolitical structures and cultural norms in which educational systems are embedded.

The cause of low-quality education and mediocre school performance cannot be laid entirely at the feet of demographic and fiscal overextension. Apart from poor management and overly centralized, ossified bureaucracies, adherence to a centuries-old institutional and cultural tradition that prizes the preservation and transmission of sacred or apodictic knowledge has had a debilitating impact on cultivating crucial learning skills indispensable to 21st-century careers.

The pedagogical emphasis on rote memorization can be traced back to the beginning of the seventh century AD, when Quranic *kuttab* schools throughout the Islamic Arab world required memorization of content and interpretation considered beyond dispute. This approach to sacred texts became a pedagogical template and model for all forms of learning up through the present moment. For example, the pedagogical emphasis on memorization continues to be a central feature of the educational system in Saudi Arabia and much of the Arab region, where the reliance on textbooks is rare and access to them is often limited.[19]

By way of example, in the 1990s, a stroll in Rabat's Jardin d'Essais park toward the end of the academic year would find it filled with dozens of university and high school students anxiously pacing as they read, recited, and memorized an entire academic year's notes for final exams. Reliance on model answers and rote memorization has hampered the kind of teaching that encourages analytical and independent thinking and embraces the collaborative problem-solving and development of technical skills suited to the requirements of the emergent global economy.

This may explain in part another indicator of overall poor performance in education in the Arab region: the reluctance of students to enter STEM fields in which traditional pedagogical dispensation is inadequate to the contemporary modes of learning and rigor STEM requires. As the *Arab Knowledge Report 2014* noted:

> Data show an imbalance in the distribution of young people enrolling at universities in scientific majors which are needed in the labour market. If we consider higher education graduates by specialisation in the Arab countries, for which data is available, we notice an imbalance between the disciplines chosen by the graduates and the needs of the society for high competences that can transform the economy in its various spheres to reliance on modern trusted knowledge. . . . We are therefore witnessing a paradox represented in a surplus of graduates from different theoretical faculties and sections with no real prospects for work, while internal labour markets lack graduates from majors that young people avoid.[20]

The causes for this have less to do with educational policy and more with deficits in the development of supporting economic structures. Much of the region suffers from a lack of qualified teachers, a profession of increasingly lower compensation and prestige. In addition, textbooks and source material are in short supply, as are modern lab equipment and information technology (IT) infrastructure. Even in those countries with capacity to provide these resources, there is often a discrepancy between what is taught in school and the skills the labor force needs.

The educational crisis is real, but educational reform in and of itself will not likely be enough to fix the problems that so many have identified because it cannot be disarticulated from the region's broader political, economic, and social crises, nor can it be separated from problems involving the distribution of technology or questions of equity and cultural values. The tension between the rate of technological change and the cultural capacity to adapt to it is not unique to the Arab world, but, perhaps as anthropologist Kevin Dwyer suggested, it is the rapidity of change coupled with a seeming incapacity to assimilate that change that makes the feeling of crisis so widespread in the region. Dwyer goes on to note that the late Moroccan sociologist Mohammed Guessous, wary of over usage of the term "crisis" ('azma), argued that constantly referring to the intractable challenges education systems faced did little to address their origins and consequences.[21]

Is Privatization the Answer?

The widespread optimism that accompanied universalizing education in the newly independent Arab states—the considerable achievements in eliminating illiteracy notwithstanding—has in recent years yielded to a growing disillusionment with public education. Schools that are increasingly underfunded and overcrowded, often staffed by teachers who are poorly trained and lacking basic materials and resources, have all led to declining confidence in public education. Consequently, private education, both formally in private institutions and informally with private tutoring, has rapidly grown in the past decade across the region, but especially among the GCC countries, where the private school market is among the largest in the world.

Growing populations, the belief that private schools offer higher-quality education and better career prospects, and GCC nationals' increased willingness to pay for education have encouraged private education's growth. All this, combined with affordable private education and large expatriate communities and international schools, make private education a greater option in the GCC.[22]

For example, in 2016 almost 58 percent of Emirati nationals sent their children to private rather than public schools, and close to 46 percent of Qataris did.[23] In Saudi Arabia, the percentage of secondary students enrolled in private schools for the same year was 17.6 percent.[24] An added attraction to the growth of private education, especially in the Gulf countries, is high return on education-sector investments, perceived by some as "recession proof" in a region where parents' investment in their children's education is expected to quadruple to $20 billion by 2020.

There are "push" factors as well, with the multiple regional conflicts and migrating refugee populations being most conspicuous among them. For example, in Lebanon, only 28 percent of Lebanese students attend public schools, which is not only a consequence of problems dating back to Lebanon's civil war but also a response to the enormous influx starting in 2012 of Syrian refugees enrolling in Lebanese schools and the enormous curricular problems this has created.[25]

In countries such as Egypt, where the growth of private schools has been less affordable and stable, there has been growing reliance on private tutoring. (A 2015 UNESCO report indicated that, contrary to expectations, private school enrollment in Egypt actually declined slightly since 2000.) As of 2015, Egyptian families were spending in excess of $2 billion a year on supplemental private lessons.[26] Region-wide, the rate of enrollment in private primary schools has been considerably higher than at the secondary level.

At the university level, similar problems with underfunding, inefficiency, and an inability to meet the needs of a growing population have resulted in governments turning to the private sector. Further, the establishment of branch campuses of Western research universities has become a salient feature in many MENA countries: Of approximately 600 universities in the region, 70 percent were established since 1990, with 40 percent of them private, accounting for 30 percent of the region's enrollments.[27]

The trend toward privatization raises several concerns, not the least of these being the uneven quality of private education. Nor has the surge in private education always been accompanied by the implementation of policies and regulatory frameworks to ensure an effective and efficient private sector. No less concerning is a shift in the past two decades from national systems of universal, free education to a mixture of public and private schools reminiscent of the colonial-era bifurcation of European and indigenous schools.

Indeed, nearly a decade ago, Oxford Analytica warned of the emergence of a two-tiered system in which equality of access is seriously compromised.[28] In a region where youth unemployment is a pressing issue, the disparity in quality between public and private education is indeed creating such a two-tiered system. As better career prospects become a chief selling point for private schools, they exist only for the minority who can afford them. To the extent that the "knowledge economy" is the future, this much is certain: Private schools are in a position to provide IT connectivity and instill technological competencies in ways with which public schools cannot compete. From a public policy vantage point, this is, needless to say, less than auspicious.

But the story—both of privatization and virtual learning—is not limited to a proliferation of private schools. Dissatisfaction with school performance and expanding web-based options have led many parents to turn to online learning. A prime example is a crowdsourced education service website, Nafham, founded by three young Egyptian technology professionals. The site has grown to 500,000 active users monthly and has expanded to offer more than 10,000 online educational videos, which, as the Nafham website indicates, "cover 75% of the [K–12 Egyptian] curriculum . . . all sorted by grade, subject and academic term."[29] Self-paced learning products in general have become a growing market in the Middle East: With a growth rate of 8.2 percent, revenues of $378.4 million in 2011 reached $560.7 million in 2016.[30] By all indications, this market will continue to expand—albeit unevenly—across the region.

The creation of a "digital divide" among—and within—Arab countries is a function of the ongoing transformations introduced by information and communications technology across the globe. As of 2014, the Middle East had exceeded the global average for internet connectivity, with 56.7 percent internet penetration in the region as a whole in 2017. The Internet World Statistics website reports that, as of March 2019, there were more than 173.5 million internet users in the 22 MENA countries, representing 62 percent of the aggregate population of the region.[31]

However, as a 2014 white paper published by the Mohammed bin Rashid School of Government reports, while a critical mass of the Arab world population has access to online service and information, apart from the relatively high connectivity of high-income countries, most of the

Arab region continues to lag behind in accessible broadband connectivity, which has become instrumental in economic growth and developmental opportunities in general and in increasing educational and skills development in particular.

That web-based learning is a small fraction of online activity in the region underscores the extent to which information and access to knowledge are no longer the exclusive preserve of educational systems and media directly under, or vulnerable to, the control of autocratic governments. The accelerated expansion of links to global knowledge and information networks is one of the two major developments that have taken place over a decade of rapid change, underscored in the *Arab Human Development Report 2016*.

The other, inextricably connected to the first, is "the high levels of dissatisfaction among youth and a growing sense among youth that they are losing control over their lives."[32] The experience of powerlessness in societies where meaningful participation in social life has been forestalled by a legacy of patriarchal values and autocratic governance looms large in the commentary of analysts who recurrently invoke the concept of "citizenship." The language of the *Arab Human Development Report 2016*, which calls for "renewed policy focus on youth development"[33] through political, economic, and social inclusion, represents much of the current critical discourse.

> Youth empowerment emphasizes the importance of participation and social inclusion. This can be achieved provided society is instilled with principles and rules of citizenship that respect all groups and their legitimate differences. The more youth are granted equitable access to education, matched with proper standards of educational attainment and achievement, hold satisfying employment and are in control of their lives, the more well equipped they will be to "reclaim" reason, assert themselves as powerful agents of change, and own the necessary debates around tomorrow's society.[34]

Muhammad Faour, formerly of the Carnegie Middle East Center, advances much the same argument, advocating education for (and education about) citizenship as essential to developing the skills "necessary to thrive in a global, democratic and competitive environment."[35] He establishes the incompatibility between highly didactic, teacher-directed pedagogy and the spirit of analytical freethinking and inquiry fostered by values of civic and political participation. Faour identifies a catch-22 dilemma here:

> Good education requires good governance, but that is lacking in the region at both the central government and local school level. Ministries of education assume a highly centralized role and continue to be dominated by authoritarian management systems. Furthermore, most ministries lack vision, appropriate strategic planning, efficient supervisory units, and competent human resources. Operating under conditions unfavorable to progress, leaders of any new initiatives will face a host of bureaucratic hurdles, including incompetent officers, many of whom are corrupt, resistant to change, or disinterested.[36]

How and where, then, do the prescribed changes begin? Surely not at a government level dominated by authoritarian management systems. But "operating under conditions unfavorable to progress," and in the face of bureaucratic hurdles and corruption, how do reform and change get initiated at the school level? And how, in the terminology of the *Arab Human Development Reports*, are such societies "instilled with principles and rules of citizenship"? The prescriptions are compelling, but their execution remains formidable in a region where by and large governments treat citizens as subjects.

Does Citizenship Matter?

The equivocal status of citizenship in the Middle East overshadows such intractable issues as outmoded pedagogy, gender inclusiveness, and obstacles to the innovations needed for emerging 21st-century economies. To be certain, the realization of citizenship as value and right in Western societies has itself been the product of a protracted historical process. But education was a necessary precondition for constituting the identity of "citizen" in the West, where the evolution of citizenship and the development of modern education systems have interlocked in distinctive ways. By contrast, in the region, where "historically there has been little opportunity to develop institutions of self-government along modern lines"[37] and the legacy of colonialism has meant a kind of heterogeneity in educational systems, the relationship between "education" and the status of "citizen" remains elusive.

The distinction is one that the late anthropologist Ernest Gellner characterized as "a kind of inverse relationship between the importance of structure and culture." Gellner argued that where communities are small, relationships are well-known, and the types of relationships are limited in number, shared culture is not a precondition for effective communication; the context of territorial proximity, shared social ties, and ongoing relationships is determinative. But modern societies, he argues, are different: This may be broadly understood in terms of the historical movement industrialization initiated from the small-scale, intimate social structure of the artisanal villages to the more socially anonymous and impersonal scale of industrialized cities. The crucial difference is that in complex, modern societies, the greater proportion of encounters are "ephemeral, non-repetitive and optional in a process of, in a manner of speaking, peasants becoming citizens."[38]

Gellner connects citizenship with not just the idea but also the function of modern education. His argument rests on two assertions. First, human beings are social creatures. Second, societies change with time. Village-size social units, after all, can no longer shape identity on a national scale. A Nuer village can still produce a Nuer, but it cannot produce an effective Sudanese citizen capable of profiting from his Sudanese citizenship. Villages do not have the resources to produce anything but potential citizens. In modern societies, raising a human being requires more than the resources of family and village; it requires an educational system.

Why? Because industrialization and modernity require it. Such was the path of modern industrialized societies: the erosion of all-embracing social structures; the emergence of an industrialized proletariat, greater mobility, and greater anonymity; the creation of a population whose members are functionally substitutable for each other; the ability of communicating by virtue of sharing a common culture, which meant the displacement of local vernaculars by national languages; and the fostering of universal literacy, in the broadest sense of the term. The only institution capable of creating cultural literacy on this scale—the scale of a nation-state—is a national education system.

Whereas the diffusion of industrialization and modernization among Western societies was an uneven process, unfolding at different rates, by contrast, there was effectively no such process in the Middle East and North Africa. In the 17th century, Arab states were weak on the international stage. Subsequent colonial rule may have reshaped boundaries, but states created by external decree struggled for legitimacy in the eyes of their populations. Claims to supranational ideologies such as pan-Arabism, Ba'athism, and variants of Islamism notwithstanding, it is not only that governance in much of the region has been largely a family affair but also that much of life is lived at the local level and continues to rely on informal kinship networks.

Is the Education System Fair?

It is through the lens of this equivocal status of citizenship that much of what frustrates education analysts in the region might be best elucidated. A case in point is the impact of gender on education. As a 2015 Brookings report titled "Unlocking the Potential of Educated Arab Women" noted in its opening page:

> For Arab women, hard-won progress in education has not earned them the economic progress they deserve. Although young women seek and succeed in tertiary education at higher rates than young men, they are far less likely to enter and remain in the job market.[39]

The figures provided in the same report are striking. While in 2014 the ratio of female-to-male tertiary enrollment in the Arab region is 108 percent (and considerably higher in some of the GCC countries and Tunisia), the unemployment rate for female youth in the region is

43.9 percent, effectively double the 22.9 percent rate for male youth. Three out of four Arab women remain outside the workforce—despite considerable progress over the past few decades in gender parity in enrollment at the primary and secondary levels as well.[40] Studies indicate no disparity in academic scores between boys and girls, and girls seem to perform academically better than boys in the GCC countries, Jordan, and Palestine, with women in Saudi Arabia outperforming men in science and math.[41] Why then has the increase in gender parity in education—particularly at the tertiary level—not been reflected in women's participation in the workforce?

The reasons are rooted in complex social, legal, and economic factors. Traditional or conservative gender roles, notions of culturally acceptable work for women, the impact of marriage and motherhood on women's participation in the workforce, and a dominant public and weak private sector figure prominently in reports and analyses of the relation between women's education and workforce participation. There exists a contradiction, particularly in Gulf nations, between those who encourage women to get an education and the socioeconomic and cultural environment that discourages their participation in the workforce. As noted in a recent World Bank report, citizens of wealthier oil-rich states can rely on state patronage for their income, in which the state becomes the "patriarch of its citizens" and traditional, conservative gender roles are reinforced.[42]

The complex social, legal, economic, and cultural factors as described in this way have different configurations across the countries in the region. Nevertheless, the stark reality of women with high levels of education having limited access to workforce participation is incommensurate with the degree and quality of social and economic participation envisioned in the values and discourse of modern citizenship. There is a different value system at play here, and, as noted, it has become embedded in the operations of states: More than a paradox, the phrase "patriarch of its citizens" might be seen as an oxymoron.

If the education system seems in some ways skewed against women, it is also tilted against the unconnected. Ubiquitous across the Middle East and North Africa, *wasta*—taking advantage of connections—can be understood as a kind of shorthand for corruption. Many recent assessments of education cite corruption's deleterious effects alongside those of authoritarianism and political stagnation. Although corruption remains notoriously difficult to define in rigorous sociological terms, the practices found in much of the Arab regions that may be characterized as "corrupt" reflect deep structural alliances between political and economic elites, beyond what is commonly recognized as opportunistic corruption.

In traditional societies, where daily interactions rely on using kin and relational networks, *wasta* is simply how social life is organized and how business gets done. It is when this mode of functioning permeates and even predominates in modern societies large enough to support an educational system that corruption as such debilitates the project of modern education.

What Is to Be Done?

It may seem counterintuitive to one's conviction in education's transformative power, but there is no educational crisis that is not, by some reckoning, also an economic, political, population, development, gender, and cultural crisis. Nor is this condition unique to the Arab region, even if the MENA region provides an extreme example. What may be distinctive about the MENA region is the extent to which vague understandings of citizenship shape the factors in which the project of education, broadly defined, is enmeshed.

This does not demean the ultimate value of "education for citizenship," which Muhammad Faour and Marwan Muasher qualify as a key 21st-century competence in a 2011 report that was especially prescient.

> Serious shortcomings in socio-political and economic systems at both the local and national levels in Arab countries will influence their citizenship education programs. Loyalty to one's ethnic or religious group is fierce; authoritarian values dominate; opportunities for participation in governance processes and decision-making are limited; and freedom of speech and belief are constrained. The resistance of hardline religious groups and authoritarian political parties to democratic values will be a major obstacle.[43]

Noting the primacy of a society's religious, political, and socioeconomic background—over home, school, and community—as the context influencing its definition of citizenship, their argument underscores a disconnect that emanates from a deeper level of social structure: between what one learns or otherwise acquires in school and the social reality that awaits him or her. There is a price to be paid for cultivating discrepant identities and discordant values in societies where former students of Émile Durkheim, Max Weber, and Pierre Bourdieu end up tending vegetable stands and a would-be student of the law comes to express—without intended irony—his disdain for things that "only exist in books."

What is to be done? To be certain, there is no uniform solution for a region divided by disparities of wealth and resources, with some areas suffering from protracted instability or catastrophic violence. The cataclysmic conflicts in Syria, Yemen, and elsewhere have devastatingly affected the well-being of children where, to cite Human Rights Watch, "children's education has become a casualty of war."[44]

In a January 2017 report, UNICEF states that the 40 percent of 1.2 million Syrian children who are refugees in Turkey and not enrolled in school are at risk of becoming "a lost generation."[45] In Yemen, where at the time of writing 460,000 children face the more severe threat of malnutrition, the number of out-of-school children has ballooned to two million.[46] Nevertheless, elsewhere, where conditions are less dire, the prospects for meaningful educational reform in the near term are not promising.

In the final pages of *Between Memory and Desire*, historian Stephen Humphreys makes the observation that, in the Arab region, "desires for the future . . . have typically been transformative rather than ameliorative; they have aimed to create a new world, not to improve the one people actually live in."[47] Certainly the events of the Arab Spring and all that has subsequently transpired have established that not all transformations are necessarily for the best or, indeed, transformative.

How would an approach to improving education look? To begin, it would look lateral and local. It would look lateral because any solution to the educational crisis will require the insights and expertise of multiple disciplines, agencies, and stakeholders and collaboration among them.

An unlikely but arguably pertinent example can be found in initiatives undertaken in the Republic of Ireland, which, while remote from the Arab region, has certain features in common. These features include a large youth population (at 33 percent of the population, the largest in Europe[48]); an enduring colonial legacy; and, most importantly, in the wake of the 2008 economic crisis, an urgent need to reinvent its educational system to better respond to existing workforce needs and to create opportunities for new ones. Ireland's National Skills Strategy 2025 model aimed "to enhance the reform of our system of education and training with a real partnership between the education sector and enterprise to provide the mix of skills needed over the next ten years and beyond."[49]

Leading the list of the strategy's objectives for 2025 are providing skills development opportunities that are relevant to the needs of learners, society, and the economy and the participation of different actors across education, private-sector training, and various parties involved in economic development. And these programs have been by and large undertaken at the local level owing to the greater flexibility, responsiveness, and accountability that this affords.

There have been examples in the Arab world where this has already taken place. A 2011 report prepared by the US Agency for International Development and the International Youth Foundation on young entrepreneurs in the West Bank cites a number of examples in which university-educated students, male and female, launched successful enterprises in a range of sectors. They did so by integrating their education with carefully designed and sustained mentorship and training components with not only regional business communities but also local and international support.

In Morocco, similar programs supporting social entrepreneurship, such as INJAZ Al-Maghreb and StartupYourLife, have been operating over the past few years with measurable success in laying the foundation for successful youth startups in diverse fields.[50] The Oman Innovation Factory, Oman's first digital manufacturing plant, has recently launched two programs sponsored by BP Oman aimed at creating in a world of rapid technological change an "ecosystem that supports passion for innovation" through educational activities and projects.[51] One of the programs involves a group of 24 Omani youth, age 18–35, working on projection mapping in soft robotics, aeroponic gardening, and wave energy.

This is complemented by a second initiative aimed at developing the innovation skills of some 500 younger students (age 9–15), encompassing such domains as composite materials and recycling. Launched with modest support by the US Department of State, the Young Tunisian Coders Academy, which teaches young people programming skills, was designed as a platform for preparing creative and innovative young brains for jobs and developing entrepreneurial skills for a global high-tech service sector.[52]

Entrepreneurship is not a panacea, and it alone will not bridge the gap between education and employment in the Arab region. But the skills and values that it requires—creativity, agility, critical thinking, problem-solving, communication, and interpersonal skills—are, as the head of research of a MENA-based entrepreneurship platform notes, not only entrepreneurial skills but "also an indispensable requisite for being an employee in any field."[53] As may be suggested by all the examples cited above, an ameliorative approach would be experimental, initially small-scale, and incremental.

It would be experimental by embracing what design thinkers refer to as "positive failure" as a tool for development. It would be small-scale by drawing inspiration through observing what others have done both in the region and beyond but, where possible, emulating their success and calibrating it to local contexts. And again, as noted above, it would put a large premium on articulations where the relatively separate spheres of "education" and "marketplace" would establish Venn diagram–like zones of institutionalized collaboration between educators and employers. And it would be incremental by aspiring to create successful practices and models one school, one project, one enterprise, and, figuratively speaking, perhaps a few underemployed vegetable vendors at a time.

Notes

1. Nader Habibi and Fatma El-Hamidi, "Why Are Egyptian Youth Burning Their University Diplomas? The Overeducation Crisis in Egypt," Brandeis University and Crown Center for Middle East Studies, September 2016, 1–10.

2. Associated Press, "'Unemployed Graduates' Set Themselves Alight in Morocco: Five out-of-Work Men Self-Immolate over Lack of Jobs in Capital Rabat," NBC News, January 19, 2012, http://www.nbcnews.com/id/46055345/ns/world_news-mideast_n_africa/t/unemployed-graduates-set-themselves-alight-morocco/#.WoX5SRPwZE4.

3. *Arab Weekly*, "Serious Education Problems Face the Arab World as Children Go Back to School," September 25, 2015, https://thearabweekly.com/serious-education-problems-face-arab-world-children-go-back-school.

4. David Leonhardt, "School Vouchers Aren't Working, but Choice Is," *New York Times*, May 2, 2017, https://www.nytimes.com/2017/05/02/opinion/school-vouchers-charters-betsy-devos.html.

5. UNESCO, "Participation in Education: Morocco," http://uis.unesco.org/country/MA.

6. Chaima Lahsini, "Unemployment: Moroccan Economy Lost More Jobs Than It Created in Q2 2017," *Morocco World News*, August 7, 2017, https://www.moroccoworldnews.com/2017/08/225482/unemployment-moroccan-economy-lost-jobs-in-q2-2017/.

7. Wagdy Sawahel, "Higher Education After the Uprisings," World University News, January 8, 2012, http://www.universityworldnews.com/article.php?story=20111222200114662.

8. Jennifer Silvi, "How Can We Tackle Youth Unemployment in the Middle East?," World Economic Forum, November 26, 2015, https://www.weforum.org/agenda/2015/11/how-can-we-tackle-youth-unemployment-in-the-middle-east/.

9. Raul Ramos, "Migration Aspirations Among NEETs in Selected MENA Countries," IZA Institute of Labor Economics, November 2017, http://ftp.iza.org/dp11146.pdf.

10. World Bank, "Fact Sheet," 2013, http://web.worldbank.org/archive/website01418/WEB/0__C-301.HTM.

11. *Economist*, "Look Forward in Anger: By Treating Youth as a Threat, Arab Rules Are Stoking the Next Revolt," August 6, 2016, https://www.economist.com/briefing/2016/08/06/look-forward-in-anger.

12. Richard Robinson and Katerina Fytatzi, "Middle East: Shift to Quality in Education Faltering," Oxford Analytica Daily Brief Service, May 20, 2008, https://dailybrief.oxan.com/Analysis/DB142781/MIDDLE-EAST-Shift-to-quality-in-education-faltering.

13. UN Development Programme, *Arab Human Development Report 2002: Creating Opportunities for Future Generations* (New York: United Nations Publications, 2002), http://hdr.undp.org/sites/default/files/rbas_ahdr2002_en.pdf.

14. UN Development Programme, *Arab Human Development Report 2016: Youth and the Prospects for Human Development in a Changing Reality* (New York: United Nations Publications, 2016), http://www.arab-hdr.org/reports/2016/english/AHDR2016En.pdf.

15. UN Development Programme, *Arab Knowledge Report 2014: Youth and Localisation of Knowledge* (New York: United Nations Publications, 2014), https://youtheconomicopportunities.org/sites/default/files/uploads/resource/Arab%20

Knowledge%20Report%202014.pdf.

16. UNESCO, "Regional Overview: Arab States," 2015, https://en.unesco.org/gem-report/sites/gem-report/files/regional_overview_AS_en.pdf.

17. UNESCO, "Education for All Movement," http://www.unesco.org/new/en/archives/education/themes/leading-the-international-agenda/education-for-all/.

18. Shanta Devarajan, "The Paradox of Higher Education in MENA," Brookings Institution, June 27, 2016, https://www.brookings.edu/blog/future-development/2016/06/27/the-paradox-of-higher-education-in-mena/.

19. William A. Rugh, "Education in Saudi Arabia: Choices and Constraints," *Middle East Policy* 9, no. 2 (June 2002): 40–55.

20. UN Development Programme, *Arab Knowledge Report 2014*, 67.

21. Kevin Dwyer, *Arab Voices: The Human Rights Debate in the Middle East* (London: Routledge, 1991).

22. Emily Perryman, "Investing in the Future: Private Education Takes off in the Middle East," JLL Real Views, September 7, 2016, https://www.jllrealviews.com/places/investing-future-private-education-takes-off-middle-east/. For individual country entries in the IndexMundi data portal, see IndexMundi, "Bahrain—School Enrollment, Secondary, Private (% of Total Secondary)," https://www.indexmundi.com/facts/bahrain/indicator/SE.SEC.PRIV.ZS. For the foreseeable future, it is anticipated that the rate of private enrollment will continue to increase.

23. US Department of Commerce, International Trade Commission, "United Arab Emirates—Education," March 15, 2019, https://www.export.gov/apex/article2?id=United-Arab-Emirates-Education.

24. Statista, "Number of High School Students in Saudi Arabia from 2013 to 2017, by School Type," May 2018, https://www.statista.com/statistics/629415/saudi-arabia-number-of-high-school-students-by-school-type/.

25. Dina Eldawy, "A Fragile Situation: Will the Syrian Refugee Swell Push Lebanon over the Edge?," Migration Policy Institute, February 21, 2019, https://www.migrationpolicy.org/article/syrian-refugee-swell-push-lebanon-over-edge; and Josephine Deeb, "In Lebanon, Even Private Schools Caught in Education Crisis," Al-Monitor, January 12, 2017, https://www.al-monitor.com/pulse/originals/2017/01/Lebanon-syrian-displaced-students-public-private-education.html.

26. Bouzou Daragahi, "Egypt's Teachers Enjoy Lucrative Sideline," *Financial Times*, October 20, 2013, https://www.ft.com/content/8ffa7a20-1af9-11e3-87da-00144feab7de.

27. Lisa Anderson, "Fertile Ground: The Future of Higher Education in the Arab World," *Social Research* 79, no. 3 (Fall 2012).

28. Robinson and Fytatzi, "Middle East."

29. Center for Education Innovations, "Nafham," http://www.educationinnovations.org/program/nafham.

30. Center for Education Innovations, "Nafham."

31. Internet World Statistics, https://www.internetworldstats.com/.

32. UN Development Programme, *Arab Human Development Report 2016*.

33. UN Development Programme, *Arab Human Development Report 2016*.

34. UN Development Programme, *Arab Human Development Report 2016*.

35. UN Development Programme, *Arab Human Development Report 2016*.

36. Muhammad Faour and Marwan Muashar, "Education for Citizenship in the Arab World: Key to the Future," Carnegie Endowment for International Peace, October 2011.

37. R. Stephen Humphreys, *Between Memory and Desire: The Middle East in a Troubled Age* (Berkeley, CA: University of California Press, 1999), 128.

38. Ernest Gellner, *Thought and Change* (Chicago: University of Chicago Press, 1964), 155.

39. Maysa Jalbout, "Unlocking the Potential of Educated Arab Women," Brookings Institution, March 12, 2015, https://www.brookings.edu/blog/education-plus-development/2015/03/12/unlocking-the-potential-of-educated-arab-women/.

40. Jalbout, *Unlocking the Potential of Educated Arab Women*.

41. Maha El-Swais, "Despite High Education Levels, Arab Women Still Don't Have Jobs."

42. Maha El-Swais, "Despite High Education Levels, Arab Women Still Don't Have Jobs."

43. Faour and Muasher, "Education for Citizenship in the Arab World," 16.

44. Human Rights Watch, "Education for Syrian Refugee Children: What Donors and Host Countries Should Do," September 16, 2016, https://www.hrw.org/news/2016/09/16/education-syrian-refugee-children-what-donors-and-host-countries-should-do.

45. UNICEF, "Over 40 Percent of Syrian Refugee Children in Turkey Missing out on Education, Despite Massive Increase in Enrollment Rates," January 19, 2017, https://www.unicef.org/press-releases/over-40-cent-syrian-refugee-children-turkey-missing-out-education-despite-massive.

46. UNICEF, "In Yemen, Children's Education Devastated After Three Years of Devastating Conflict," March 27, 2018, https://www.unicef.org/mena/press-releases/yemen-childrens-education-devastated-after-three-years-escalating-conflict.

47. Humphreys, *Between Memory and Desire*, 27.

48. IDA Ireland, "Workforce and Demographics," https://www.idaireland.com/invest-in-ireland/ireland-demographics.

49. Damien English and Jan O'Sullivan, *Ireland's National Skills Strategy 2025*, Department of Education and Skills, https://www.education.ie/en/Schools-Colleges/Services/National-Skills-Strategy/.

50. INJAZ Al-Maghreb, http://injaz-morocco.org/en/; and StartupYourLife, https://www.start-up.ma/organisme/startupyourlife/.

51. Adelle Geronimo, "Oman Innovation Factory Launches Programmes for Young Inventors," Tahawultech.com, December 21, 2017, https://www.tahawultech.com/news/oman-innovation-factory-young-inventors/.

52. Young Tunisian Coders Academy, https://www.facebook.com/YTCAcademyTunisia/.

53. Sarah Alaoui, "Developing Youth Entrepreneurship in Morocco," Al-Jazeera, August 29, 2015, https://www.aljazeera.com/indepth/opinion/2015/08/developing-youth-entrepreneurship-morocco-150829100520007.html.

6

What Will It Take to Repair Middle Eastern Economies?

BILAL WAHAB

The Middle East is among the world's richest regions in natural resources, but despite the Persian Gulf's ostentatious oil wealth, as a whole, the region teeters on the economic precipice. East Asia, South Asia, and even Latin America—once peers in business and development—have left the Middle East in the dust. Rather than embark on slow and steady growth, Middle Eastern economies remain trapped by boom-and-bust cycles of economic development, often a case of two steps forward, two steps back. Environmental concerns, such as desertification and fresh water shortages, add another layer of complexity. But other regions have overcome similar obstacles to thrive. Why has the Middle East failed so spectacularly to do so?

It is easy to blame the Middle East's democratic deficit, but that is not enough to explain the entire problem. After all, China and Singapore have seen exponential economic growth in the past half century without embracing democracy. And South Korea's and Taiwan's economic engines developed long before either completed their democratic transitions.

What then has stymied the Middle East's economic development? There is no single answer. Oil-rich countries have fallen prey to rentier state dynamics, but corruption ravages rich and poor states alike. Decades of socialism and command economies have taken their toll. So too has the Arab-Israeli conflict and myriad others. The business climate in many countries repels rather than attracts investment, but even when investors dip their toes into the Middle East market, the lack of a stable, developed middle class and indigenous capacity exacerbated by decades of labor importation continue to impede growth.

The Problem of Oil

In 2013, University of California, Los Angeles, political scientist Michael Ross published his seminal book *The Oil Curse: How Petroleum Wealth Shapes the Development of Nations.*[1] He showed that petro-states are 50 percent more likely to be ruled by autocrats than resource-poor countries and twice as likely to experience civil wars. Because oil-rich states spend significant shares of their national wealth on armaments, the use of force is too often the default response to political conflict. In Algeria, Bahrain, Saddam Hussein–era Iraq, and Sudan, the state has crushed social and political unrest with brute force. Syrian oil funded not only Bashar al-Assad's post-2011 crackdown but also the Islamic State's short-lived caliphate.

Subsequent events have only affirmed Ross' thesis. Democracy has expanded across the globe since 1980. Despite recent backsliding, democracy has made great gains in Eastern Europe, Latin America, Sub-Saharan Africa, and even East Asian countries, such as South Korea and Taiwan. Broadly speaking, however, oil-dependent countries have been the outliers.

Vast petroleum resources in the Middle East have enabled many states to resist reform. States such as Algeria, Iraq, and the oil-rich Persian Gulf emirates have grown dependent on oil or gas income, which in turn has created a dynamic nourishing patronage over economic growth.[2] Foreign aid has created a similar dynamic in states such as Egypt, Lebanon, and the Palestinian Authority. In each case, the result ossifies autocratic but brittle governance.

Not only do such dynamics stymie democracy (admittedly not a concern for the Gulf monarchies), but, when elections do occur, they also unleash patronage politics and competition over public resources and become a test of, as the University of Oxford's Paul Collier quips, "survival of the fattest."[3] That is why when autocracies find oil, democratization becomes less likely.

The nationalization of oil industries, especially in the 1970s, has only augmented the resource curse in the Middle East. Oil revenues, which economists call rent, flowed into government coffers. Studies assert that large resource rents from oil and gas lead government officials to take the easier short-term path of seeking even more revenue from natural resources rather than embarking on pro-growth policies that would provide longer-term stability.[4]

Rent also breeds inefficiency. As a fraction of their economies, petro-state governments are on average 50 percent larger than oil-poor ones.[5] Compared to governments that rely on a solid tax base, petroleum rents create top-down flows of wealth and power. Moreover, the government sector benefits disproportionately more from oil rents and grows more quickly than the rest of the economy.

Although, on average, the oil sector constitutes only 19 percent of the economy, oil rents fund 54 percent of state budgets.[6] Against low extraction costs that averaged below $10 per barrel in the Middle East, no other industry can rival the return on investment. That is why, on autopilot, the petroleum industry tends to crowd out other industries and deepens not only the government's but also the whole economy's dependence on oil.

The danger of overdependence, of course, is that the price of oil is notoriously volatile. Crude was $10 per barrel in June 1999, $145 in June 2008, and $45 in June 2017. In June 2014 alone, oil prices fell 40 percent.[7] The Organization of the Petroleum Exporting Countries (OPEC) seeks to set prices, but political differences among members, cheating, and the growing number of non-OPEC producers erodes its ability to do so.

There are other dangers as well. Oil-rich, low-population states can be tempting targets for indebted states, which seek an easy way to fill their coffers without undertaking hard reforms. Saddam Hussein ordered Iraqi forces into Kuwait ostensibly over an oil drilling dispute, but, in reality, the aim was to loot Iraq's tiny neighbor to replenish Baghdad's treasury and patronage networks.[8]

Governments have been slow to adjust their oil-dependent economies. Four decades ago, Saudi Minister of Oil and Mineral Resources Ahmed Zaki Yamani warned, "The Stone Age did not end for lack of stone, and the Oil Age will end long before the world runs out of oil."[9] And yet, it took Saudi Arabia decades more to begin serious efforts to diversify its economy, and even then, the success of diversification remains unclear.

Plans for building a broad-based economy are undermined by complacency during fat years and the need to increase spending at the expense of investment in low years. The problem is not just political inertia. Due to the influx of foreign currency, exchange rates inflate in favor of national denominations. This in turn makes goods easier to import than produce.

The problem is that the energy industry is capital- and technology- rather than labor-intensive. Oil accounts for more than 80 percent of Saudi Arabia's revenues,[10] but the industry employs only 1.6 percent of the workforce.[11] Governments then hire excess employees only to provide jobs, even if they are not productive.

When oil prices crash, ability to absorb the shock is limited. Saudi Arabia and the United Arab Emirates (UAE) cushion the blow with sovereign wealth funds, which they can tap to fill budget gaps, but they still have implemented some unpopular austerity measures. The Iraqi government managed to muddle through the perfect storm of low oil prices and the Islamic State challenge by slashing expenditures, deficit spending, and borrowing, but Iraq's Kurdistan Regional Government remains months behind in salary payments due to its bloated civil servant class and foreign creditors. However, simply cutting payrolls can be risky. The International Monetary Fund curbed its pressure on the Iraqi government to slash subsidies and reduce the size of government before the 2018 elections, which risks a populist backlash that could upend reform.

The Problem of Corruption

Corruption blights the Middle East and North Africa (MENA) from Morocco to Iran and from Turkey to Yemen. In 2015, 50 million people in the MENA region—nearly one in three—had to pay a bribe to access public services.[12] While terrorist attacks that dominate headlines may affect dozens or hundreds, corruption affects millions. Corruption fuels patronage networks, which in turn help ruling groups maintain power and resist reforms.

One of the problems hampering the fight against corruption is that legislative definitions of corruption are far more permissive of practices ordinary people would find corrupt. Many state legal codes lag behind the complexity of corruption in modern governments and state-business relations. For instance, while clear on bribery and embezzlement, Iraq's penal code is ambivalent toward more damaging practices such as conflict of interest and nepotism, both of which have exacerbated the patronage networks that blight the country.[13] No longer culturally sanctioned, the public is revolting against such corrupt practices.

Of the 21 Middle East states measured, 19 scored very low on Transparency International's 2017 Corruption Perceptions Index, which captures levels of corruption in the public sector. Transparency International concluded, "In the absence of separation of powers, and without strong and transparent public institutions and accountability mechanisms, the introduction of anti-corruption laws and regulations becomes more lip service than real and much needed political and institutional reform."[14]

Some improvements and new legislation curbing corruption have been introduced. Algeria and Tunisia, for instance, approved comprehensive anti-corruption frameworks, including greater transparency, a code of conduct for public workers, and protections for whistleblowers. Palestinian civil society campaigned against *wasta*, the ubiquitous practice of nepotism and intermediation in the Middle East.[15] To attract business and reduce opportunities for bribery, Egypt cut down the number of procedures to register a business from 19 to three.[16] The majority of Middle Eastern states have either signed or ratified the United Nations Convention Against Corruption and developed legal frameworks about bribery, money laundering, and public procurement. To support the UN Convention, the Arab Region Parliamentarians Against Corruption was formed in 2004.[17] Nevertheless, complex and confusing legal codes continue to enable loopholes for evasion.

Oil, of course, exacerbates corruption. Oil industries are notoriously opaque. It is often easier to learn about the private dalliances and extravagance of oil princes and the nouveau riche than about the true reserves of various oil fields. Oil and gas contracts are prone to loopholes and kickbacks.

Moreover, since the sector is often highly centralized in an oil ministry or national company, revenues are easier to hide from the public. By turning national oil companies into personal banks and off-budget accounts, the dictators of Iraq and Libya used national wealth for self-enrichment at their people's expense. Even when the wealth does trickle down, it often does so in a fashion that nurtures patronage networks based on nepotism and cronyism, as in Algeria, Azerbaijan, or Iraq.

The Problem with Foreign Aid

Just as oil can grease corruption, so too can foreign aid. Traditionally, the United States gives military and economic aid to foster alliances, promote democracy, and address humanitarian concerns.[18] But since 1946, the United States has given Middle Eastern countries nearly $300 billion with little to show in either democracy or stability.[19]

This should not be surprising. The dilemma of foreign aid is not the amount of money given but how it is dispersed. In effect, foreign aid passes through a pork-barrel buffet of loyalist rewards before reaching its intended organizations, many of which are government-operated non-governmental organizations. Likewise, private-sector aid will often go to a dedicated regime ally who controls a disproportionate amount of enterprises to ensure regime loyalty.

The United States normally gives aid directly to foreign governments, which in turn promise to distribute it in mutually agreed on ways. Often, opaque governments divert aid. But, even when they do not, money is fungible, and aid can cover for other funds that top officials embezzle.

Hilton Root outlines his case against current foreign aid practices in his insightful book *Alliance Curse: How America Lost the Third World*.[20] He argues that authoritarian regimes are more concerned with the security of their regimes than with the well-being of civil society or the people. Therefore, instead of dispersing funds among civil society or independent firms, Middle Eastern governments are more likely to give funds to cronies and regime loyalists. Civil society atrophies when underfunded and neglected. Rather than strengthen civil society, then, foreign aid can actually strengthen its opponents.[21]

But despite its shortcomings, foreign aid remains a significant foreign policy tool, one that is evolving. To improve aid's effectiveness, the US Congress in 2004 created the Millennium Challenge Corporation (MCC), an independent aid agency. The MCC forced countries—those in the MENA region such as Algeria, Jordan, Morocco, and Tunisia—to compete across 17 policy performance indicators to qualify for assistance ensuring greater progress in good governance, human resource investments, and economic freedom. Each recipient country identified its growth priorities and lead in implementation.[22] Nevertheless, the traditional model of foreign assistance persists, not only from the United States but also more broadly from wealthier countries and the United Nations, and it continues to distort the economies of certain countries, much as oil does.

The Problem of Labor Importation

Many Middle Eastern states, especially the oil-rich Persian Gulf emirates, depend on imported labor. Qatar, Saudi Arabia, and the UAE consistently rank among the countries with the highest proportion of immigrant laborers as a percentage of the total population. Some of these workers are Arabs from poorer countries such as Egypt and Jordan, but a significant portion come from Asian countries such as Bangladesh, India, and Pakistan.[23] The International Labour Organization estimated that as of 2015 there were as many as 32 million immigrant workers in Arab states.[24]

In many Persian Gulf countries, an unspoken social contract exists in which citizens receive a strong social welfare program in exchange for political quiescence. Part of this contract is the expectation that the state will provide jobs for locals regardless of skill set or capabilities.[25] Often, the burden of providing jobs falls on the public sector, which produces overloaded bureaucracies where governments pay employees to stare at stacks of paper. Failure to provide these jobs can have disastrous effects, as the Arab Spring demonstrated.

Immigrant laborers pose a theoretical threat to low-skilled, low-motivated natives. The UAE's private sector is 90 percent immigrant workers, leaving the bulk of UAE natives' roles in the public sector.[26] Certain countries have learned work-arounds for the burden of low-skilled workers by turning passports into commodities. In Kuwait and Saudi Arabia, only citizens are allowed to own land, so retail stores must have local stakeholders to operate.[27] Simply put, this shifts the burden of unemployed locals to another country's private sector.

The most significant effect of immigrant labor on local economies is remittances. Most immigrant workers, knowing their stay is temporary, send back as much of their salaries as possible to family members in their home countries. In 2014, these workers remitted an estimated $95.8 billion from Kuwait, Oman, Qatar, Saudi Arabia, and the UAE.[28] That year, in individual rankings, Saudi Arabia was second globally for total remitted dollars, and the UAE was sixth, with the United States in first place and the Russian Federation, Switzerland, and Germany occupying the third, fourth, and fifth positions respectively.[29]

Remittances account for 14.6 percent of West Bank and Gaza gross domestic product (GDP) and 12.3 percent of Yemen's GDP. Across the Arab world, remittances still account for a significant 2.2 percent of GDP.[30] While in theory, outward cash flows should harm the host country, the reality is murkier. In 2017, the $13.7 billion of remittances sent by Bangladeshi workers primarily in Saudi Arabia had a minimal effect on the kingdom's $646 billion GDP.[31] While they inject necessary cash into the local economy, remittances impede female participation in the workforce in countries such as Egypt, which sends male workers abroad to send back remittances.[32]

That said, while host countries seek to remain homogenous and prevent an underclass of permanent immigrants, they arguably miss untapped potential. If managerial-class workers could move their families to host countries and settle more permanently, they would be more likely to invest in property or local industry, a benefit that might offset some obvious social challenges. The question then for Gulf economies is whether any mechanism can encourage local investment so that immigrant workers can have a more beneficial, rather than neutral, effect on the economy.

The Problem with Reliance on Subsidies

Subsidies, a government intervention ostensibly meant to benefit the poor or specific industries by suppressing prices, are corrosive to Middle Eastern economies. They serve political or social, as compared to economic, objectives. And while Arabs, Iranians, and Turks like cheap bread, gasoline, or electricity, such subsidies are counterproductive as they drain government budgets and perpetuate poverty and unemployment. While populations quickly come to view subsidies as entitlements, subsidies create deadweight loss whereby their costs surpass their benefits.

In Egypt, bread subsidies alone accounted for 10 percent of GDP in 2014. Coupled with those for fuel, spending on subsidies accounted for

90 percent of the country's deficit spending in the 2011–12 budget.[33] In comparison, Egypt spent a mere 3.75 percent of its GDP on education in 2008 and similar amounts in 2011 and 2013, down from an all-time high of 5.6 percent in 1983.[34] As a percentage of government spending, subsidies, grants, and other nonrepayable social transfers accounted for 41.7 percent in 2014, a sharp increase from 6.3 percent in 1994.[35] Such trends extend to the Middle East writ large, where subsidies and transfers accounted for 32 percent of government expenses in 2010, according to the World Bank.[36]

According to Michael Ross, fuel subsidies are a hallmark of autocratic regimes, which spend more on suppressing fuel prices than do democracies.[37] In Saudi Arabia, gasoline is cheaper than bottled water. Fuel subsidies account for most of the unproductive government spending. According to the International Monetary Fund, energy subsidies cost Arab countries in 2015 an estimated $117 billion, 5.5 percent of their GDP and more than a quarter of global energy subsidies.[38] In Iran, fuel and electricity subsidies amounted to 20 percent of Iran's 2007–08 GDP, equivalent to $3,275 of revenue per family of four.[39]

Fuel subsidies, however, can reverberate in negative ways. They primarily benefit the wealthy—one needs a car, if not many, to benefit—and they can also fuel corruption. Iran's Islamic Revolutionary Guard Corps makes billions of dollars each year selling subsidized fuel at marked-up prices. Rather than benefit ordinary Iranians, therefore, the fuel subsidies become a mechanism to transfer money from the central bank to the military.

To appease their populations during the 2011 Arab Spring, almost all Middle Eastern governments extended new subsidies to their citizenry.[40] But while subsidies are popular and easy to set up, eliminating them is trickier. In April 2010, demonstrations in Kyrgyzstan against high gasoline prices escalated into mass protests that toppled the country's president.[41]

Not even Saudi Arabia has been immune. Against the backdrop of oil price crashes in the 1980s, the Saudi government experimented with raising taxes and cutting subsidies. The result was extensive public protests that forced the government to revoke both measures.[42] This phenomenon was similar to Egypt's experience with cutting subsidies in 1977, which also provoked bread riots throughout the country.[43] Even today, the Saudi government has struggled to raise fuel prices to international levels as part of its plan to reduce dependence on oil. To augment public discord, the Saudi government is planning a benefit program to pay low- and middle-income Saudis to help their adjustment before price hikes come into effect.[44]

Middle Eastern governments mainly spend oil revenues and foreign aid to finance subsidies. Such revenues are almost the antithesis of taxes. If taxation promotes accountable governance, subsidies support co-optation of the public and its acquiescence to the government. Subsidies also drain money that might otherwise be used to invest and develop.

Low oil prices have created incentives for subsidy reforms simply because Middle Eastern governments no longer have the cash to delay much-needed reforms. For example, as part of Egypt's 2016–17 budget, energy subsidies were cut from 61 billion Egyptian pounds to 35 billion ($3.94 billion).[45]

There is no magic formula about how to extricate economies from decades of subsidies. Transparency and timing matter.[46] To blunt the poor's pain, governments often extend targeted benefits, such as cash transfers, to those most in need as they cut broader subsidy programs.[47]

Universal cash transfers are one popular policy prescription to wean populations off subsidies.[48] Coupled with other reform steps, such as communication campaigns and raising prices gradually, cash transfers have helped Iran, Jordan, and Morocco tackle the disruptive task of cutting energy subsidies.[49] Such measures, however, require effective governance to identify, for example, the most vulnerable who need cash transfers. Cutting food subsidies hurts inflation rates in a country such as Egypt, where food products account for 40 percent of its consumer price index. Hence, gradual phasing, accompanied with welfare spending and income redistribution measures, would be necessary.[50]

The Problem of Business Climate and Job Creation

Singapore shows democracy is not always necessary to thrive economically. While Middle Eastern leaders believe they too can follow that model, they often miss two important steps: maintaining relatively even playing fields for business and upholding contract law. Hence, when Egypt, Turkey, and the Iraqi Kurdistan region sought economic development absent commitment to a level business playing field, the result was crony capitalism.

The state-business relationship tightened, and real or perceived corruption worsened. Cracks quickly developed, and promised outside investment dried up. The simple fact is this: When a robust and entrepreneurial private sector operates on a level playing field, it provides the services that society demands, but when a narrow, unaccountable elite rigs the rules, the result is concentration of wealth absent the goods and services the public desires.

The dichotomy between inclusive and exclusive institutions is important.[51] Inclusive economic institutions—for example, labor unions and civil society organizations—promote sustainable economic development, while extractive institutions fester on rent-seeking and cronyism.[52]

The Arab world continues to suffer from a cocktail of destabilizing factors; the region is burdened with the world's highest youth unemployment rate (30 percent of people age 15–24 are unemployed) while having one of the world's fastest population growth rates.[53] Government job creation has been unable to keep up with rising labor demand. Private-sector job creation has remained anemic; meanwhile, cronyism suppresses outside investment.

The way forward for job creation is to increase productivity through diversification and adopt modern technologies and organizational structures.[54] In addition to promoting small- and medium-sized enterprises, these countries should attract multinational corporations given their positive ripple effect on local economies; they create demand for local businesses and offer more training and upward mobility than family-owned enterprises can. Larger US and UK companies are also bound by national anti-corruption laws, such as the US Foreign Corrupt Practices Act, and so are less likely to indulge in practices that hinder the broader economy.

Enabling privatization remains a challenge. Socialism ravaged the Middle East in the latter half of the 20th century. Arab economies have historically been state-centered and hostile to foreign direct investment. Being the only familiar economic system, the elite and public often default to fixing the state-centric economy rather than tolerate the pains of transitioning to free markets. Protectionism shielded bloated state-owned industries from real competition. So long as political elites maintained their own local monopolies and could grow wealthy, they did not care that their national economies had grown increasingly moribund.

While necessary, privatization can catalyze corruption if it is mishandled. Politically connected elites use their inside track to acquire state-owned enterprises at fire-sale prices. In Russia, President Vladimir Putin's "associates" oversee state corporations. As Russia transitioned toward a market economy, privatization at the hands of well-connected insiders of state-owned assets gave rise to a new class of oligarchs. Similarly, real estate market privatization in the Iraqi Kurdistan region and preferential access granted to the politically connected resulted in a real estate bubble.[55] The US government has long expressed concern about the linkage between political leaders and private family businesses in the region.[56] Such a nexus between privatization and corruption feeds into an existing reticence toward the much-needed market reforms in the Middle East.[57]

The Problem of the Middle Class

The middle class is a notoriously nebulous concept, but, generally, it relates to the economic security that prevents one from falling below the poverty line, which, of course, is different from state to state. In the Middle East, the middle class is a conundrum. Throughout the 1960s, 1970s, and 1980s, it was part of the ruling coalition among authoritarians and monarchies alike.[58] The middle class provided a large regime support base and was an integral part in stabilizing the economy. It was often disproportionately comprised of state employees rather than members of the private sector.

For the purposes of regime security, controlling the middle class made sense because it was most likely to organize and petition for political change. However, state control of the middle class stagnated economic growth by limiting the middle class to state structures and revenues and not allowing it the freedom to provide services where the state was not the most efficient provider. In petro-states, government-controlled middle classes are at the mercy of oil markets and may find that their salaries and subsidies need to be cut to continue funding other projects such as national defense.

In the 1990s, the middle class began to dissolve, and inequality rose, since growth was not accompanied by income distribution policies that would generate jobs.[59] Citizens disillusioned by the promise of public-sector employment and unable to advance in society without necessary prerequisites, such as *wasta*, were forced to protest against the government for more jobs and economic opportunities.[60] Cries of "bread and social justice" underlined the people's economic hardship. The erosion of the middle class and its quality of life was the real driving factor behind the Arab Spring uprisings, rather than slow growth or inequality.[61]

To bolster the middle class, governments must reduce the job market's reliance on the public sector. Chronic unemployment was one of the most cited concerns by protesters during the Arab Spring partly due to the lack of private-sector firms that could hire workers in an overextended public sector.[62] Allowing the private sector to grow will compromise the state's stifling grip on enterprises, but if events like the Arab Spring are likely without reforms, then the safer bet for regimes is to reform and allow more workers to be employed outside government control.

Ending subsidies and monopolies will also benefit the middle class by forcing industries to become more efficient and hire educated, upwardly mobile workers. Reducing state inefficiency will also bring the economic benefit of freeing the state to fund development projects within their own countries, such as the King Abdullah Economic City in Saudi Arabia.[63] Funding development projects instead of subsidies could still placate the population through projects that grow the economy, raise standards of living, and provide jobs, even without lowering bread or cooking oil prices.

Easier social mobility could increase the speed of middle-class creation, although this requires modification of several social practices, most notably *wasta*. The use of family connections almost always guarantees that jobs do not go to the most qualified and permanently disenfranchises those who might otherwise join the middle class. Unlike *wasta*, inclusive and impersonal institutions drive economic growth and state stability.

The Problems of Women in the Middle East

Corollary to middle-class empowerment are prospects for women's employment. The Middle East has a mixed record on female employment. Female education and literacy has increased along with the world average, but translating education into employment and economic productivity has not proved easy.

Female education has increased in recent years. The number of women on campuses has increased and now surpasses the amount of men in secondary education in more prosperous Middle Eastern countries. Female literacy has also reached approximately 80 percent, matching the 2015 UN human development goal.

Economic theory dictates that higher education will logically lead to more economic opportunity and empowerment, but this is not the first time the Middle East has flown in the face of economic or political theory. A 2012 Gallup poll showed that two-thirds of Arab women were out of the workforce.[64] Although the gender gap is shrinking in sectors such as access to health care and education, it stays largely unchanged in the economic sphere. Average unemployment for women with postsecondary education in the region remains over 50 percent after one year of job search.[65] Similarly, and regardless of education level, the gap between women and men with a full-time job as a percentage of the population is 23 percent, the highest in the world.[66] The World Bank refers to this puzzling phenomenon as "the Arab Paradox."[67]

The World Economic Forum's Global Gender Gap Report ranks the Middle East above only South Asia on economic opportunities for women. Moreover, progress toward parity remains extremely slow; at current rates it would take 153 years to close the overall gender gap. Less than 7 percent of women hold managerial positions in Egypt, Pakistan, Saudi Arabia, and Yemen.[68] Such gender gaps aggravate the issue of reservation wages and partially explain why women choose not to look for work. In instances when the opportunity cost of low-wage employment is not raising a family, women often prefer to stay home and raise families if their husbands have high enough wages to support a family. Moreover, no Arab country has legislated the prohibition of sexual harassment in the workplace.[69]

States with no or insignificant oil, such as Lebanon, Morocco, and Tunisia, have greater female participation in their workforces, elections, and parliaments than their oil-rich neighbors Libya, Qatar, and Saudi Arabia. This is in part because of large government spending, which fosters patriarchy and reduces the need for women to enter the workforce. And those who work tend to do it for the government, as in Jordan, where 82 percent of women's jobs are in the public sector.[70]

Moreover, through Dutch Disease, oil wealth crowds out export-oriented industries such as textiles, which are more prone to hiring women. Consider Algeria and Morocco. The neighboring former French colonies have similar Muslim populations (35 million). Both granted women suffrage after their independence in the mid-20th century. However, Algeria's oil income per capita in 2002 was $1,037 versus none in Morocco. The latter's clothing export per capita was $94, compared to only $9 in Algeria. Female labor force participation in Morocco was 26 percent (non-agriculture sector for 2000) compared to 12 percent in Algeria. By many accounts, Algeria should have performed better on women's rights since it is a socialist republic; Morocco is a conservative monarchy.[71] Morocco's industry-based economy attracts greater women participation than oil-rich Algeria.

For those women who do work, cultural norms specify the professions acceptable to women: nurses, teachers, clerical workers, and other similar jobs. Employment theoretically competes with women's ability to bear and raise children, and the previously mentioned careers have short hours, high respectability, and plenty of leave to raise children. The UAE's public sector is 60 percent female due to its short hours, long vacation time, and forced retirement at age 49.[72]

If women want to become self-employed and start their own businesses, acquiring loans is difficult as women do not usually have the required collateral to receive bank loans. A September 2017 World Bank report on Jordan noted that, due to discriminatory hiring practices and lack of access to capital, women often start home businesses, which provide more income without competing with child-rearing expectations.[73] Unfortunately, this has a deleterious effect on the economy as these informal businesses are not taxable because they are not reported. In other words, female discrimination in the Middle East not only limits economic growth but also actively removes money from the formal economy.

Several simple changes could be made that not only allow women to be more employed and employable but also maximize the economic benefits of allowing women to work. The first proposal is opening more profitable careers to women. Voluntary unemployment due to lower reservation wages is one of the major impediments to increased female employment.

Rather than simply mandating raised wages for female employees, allowing women to contribute to fields that are more profitable will solve the problem without creating further government involvement in the private sector. This suggestion may run counter to the societal limits on female employment, but economic data on the benefits of female employment will absolutely validate compromising cultural practices.

Second, raising retirement ages in public-sector jobs would allow women to have longer careers and contribute more to the economy and their personal careers. This suggestion has already been followed to a certain degree. The UAE proposed a law in February 2017 that increased the required retirement age by one year. Obviously, more drastic measures than a one-year increase are required to significantly expand economic benefits, but progress is already being made in the proper direction.

Third, lowering capital requirements on loans for female businesses could increase female business ownership, which in turn allows the state to tax income from these businesses. Formalizing aspects of the informal economy that are economically beneficial empowers employed women and allows the state to benefit.

Finally, imposing affirmative action–style requirements for company employees and university STEM programs would lend the might of the law to enhance female economic participation. While this might be the most economically viable move, higher numbers of female secondary-educated degree holders would increase the likelihood that more employees would become college educated. More females in STEM fields is not specifically a Middle Eastern issue but nonetheless could contribute to women filling more technical jobs and earning higher wages.

During a 2007 visit to Saudi Arabia, Microsoft founder Bill Gates was asked if the kingdom could become one of the top 10 economies in the world by 2010. Gates responded by saying that the kingdom would not get anywhere close when half its talent cannot work.[74] Female economic participation is not difficult to increase and could provide massive benefits to Middle Eastern countries. The question is not whether Middle Eastern countries should increase female participation, but whether they can stomach it.

That said, while a strong economy absent democracy is possible, it can be difficult to have democracy without economic liberalization. Modernization theorists, such as Seymour Lipset and Samuel Huntington, argue that a linear relationship exists between economic modernization and democratization. They suggest that the industrialization, urbanization, literacy, transportation, and communication inherent in a strong economy creates enough complexity in the system to impede the central command inherent to autocracy.[75] Economic development, typically measured by increases in GDP, could be misleading, they argue, since not all economic growth is equal as far as political impact goes.

Not that the economic data shared by closed or opaque autocratic governments are necessarily accurate. GDP growth stemming from petroleum exports, for example, is qualitatively different than growth arising from a more diversified economy, as it does not require or result in the emergence of a middle-class characteristic of democracy. Diversification is necessary even absent democracy, as the sustained development of the resource-poor Asian Tigers and economic comparison to their former Middle Eastern and African peers demonstrates.

The Problem of Trade Unions

Trade unions represent a cornerstone of suffrage and lobbying the government for better working conditions. In the Middle East, trade unions have a mixed history in their function and relations to the state. Trade unions represent a tool of social control and worker coercion in many single-party republics. Often, Middle East states will recognize only one union, and the state will expect union leaders to keep workers under control, as was the situation in Egypt until the Arab Spring.

In promoting a middle class, trade unions offer the opportunity to demand better wages, working hours, and conditions. These rights are integral in helping produce a laboring middle class and fostering the development of industry outside government control. Middle Eastern trade unions rarely operate free from the central government. Governments that use unions to control the populace do not allow such promotion and, therefore, are less likely to promote middle-class-friendly policies. Many Gulf Cooperation Council (GCC) countries banned trade unions outright until the past decade because they feared workers lobbying for better work conditions or powerful trade unions agitating against governments.[76]

Whether trade unions have actually improved circumstances in Gulf countries is questionable. Here, Qatar is a compelling example. The number of migrant worker deaths could reach 4,000 before completion of the World Cup stadium and infrastructure projects in 2022.[77] Other countries have more tolerant approaches to labor unions, such as Tunisia, where the government expects cooperation from union leadership, but leadership ultimately has a degree of freedom from the government.

However, change may be coming. In Egypt, for years, the government allowed only the Egyptian Trade Federation Union (ETFU) to exist, and all other unions were illegal. Union leadership did not allow workers to attend protests and rallies, so a new union was formed. The Egyptian Federation of Independent Trade Unions was created in 2011 from the members of the ETFU and allowed its members to take part in protests, substantially increasing the amount of people present during protests.

In Tunisia, the Tunisian General Labor Union (UGTT) was under control of the Ben Ali government despite its independent status. After Mohammed Bouazizi's death, the union cut all ties with the government and organized its members to protest the government. The UGTT was part of the Tunisian National Dialogue Quartet, which won the Nobel Peace Prize in 2015 for "its decisive contribution to the building of a pluralistic democracy in Tunisia in the wake of the Jasmine Revolution of 2011."[78] These two examples showcase that despite significant government constraints, labor unions can break limitations to promote workers' prosperity.

Iraq has a long history of trade unions, although Saddam Hussein banned them in 1987.[79] While Article 22 of the 2005 Iraqi constitution guarantees "the right to form and join unions and professional associations," the parliament has yet to modernize and update the legal codes that govern such unions, so the cabinet still regulates them.[80]

In Iraq and the Iraqi Kurdistan region, such unions and syndicates are politicized and co-opted by ruling political parties. Party-controlled unions and nongovernmental organizations are always better funded than truly independent organizations. These party-dominated unions are among the loudest voices against privatization, as manifested by the strikes and protests of Basra oil workers and unions against the return of international oil companies.[81] Too often, the government avoids the headache of dealing with workers by deferring the modernization of state-owned enterprises.[82]

The Problem of Disruptive Technology

The region is facing technological penetration and disruption that present potential opportunities for closing the skills and employment gaps. The Middle East is catching up with the world in the realm of information and communications technology. A slew of technological companies—software development, e-commerce, and online and mobile phone services—have mushroomed in the region. A tech-savvy demographic, dubbed "the Arab Digital Generation," accounts for 40 percent of the region's population.[83] Between 2006 and 2016, data flows between the Middle East and the world increased more than 150-fold, according to a report by McKinsey & Company.[84] But digitization among countries in the region remains uneven: high in GCC countries and low in conflict states, such as Syria and Yemen.

There is a prize to consider. Research by McKinsey & Company estimates that if the region's potential 160 million digital users by 2025 were to form a unified digital market across the Middle East, they could contribute 3.8 percent in GDP annually, a sizable $95 billion. Digital adoption and growth are mutually reinforcing.[85]

Unlike social reticence toward some measures such as privatization, the Arab attitude toward internet access is quite positive. One survey indicated that 90 percent of young citizens with internet access think such connectivity would help them find jobs and create business.[86] Enabling the younger generation to tap into the digital marketplace might make governments see the youth bulge less as a liability and more as an asset.

Coupled with and feeding into tech-enabled entrepreneurship is improving and updating the region's education system.[87] In recent decades, the Arab world has made significant progress in education. For example, universal primary access has increased by 10 percent and youth and adult literacy by 22 percent, true for both genders.[88]

The gap lies in the quality of education and its mismatch with skills the market needs. Rote learning, standardized tests, and university degrees designed for the public sector do not match the private sector's ever-changing skill needs. Literacy and numeracy alone are no longer adequate; to meet market needs, youth need to "demonstrate adaptability, creativity, and above all aptitude for learning to learn—autonomously and continuously."[89]

Governments and businesses, too, lag behind this fast-paced technological trend and have yet to embrace full digital adoption. Despite ambitious plans, only 6 percent of the public lives under a "digitized, smart government."[90] Likewise, business digitization faces inadequate funding available to startups and the workforce. Alignment of the region's governance structures and ease of market entry, skilled and talented labor, and access to capital is needed. For example, a 2013 survey of the challenges facing startups in the MENA region showed that technology companies have greater access to angel investors, incubators, and venture capitals than funding from commercial banks.[91]

Conclusions

One way to circumvent the loyalist reward program is to invest directly in businesses and cut out the government middleman. Directly investing in nongovernmental enterprise and giving international approval to private competition can change the dynamic in Middle Eastern countries and actually promote liberal economies.

Within the World Bank Group, the International Finance Corporation acts as a private investor to create markets "where they are needed most."[92] If governments could act as private investors like the International Finance Corporation, skip the handouts integral to authoritarian regimes' support networks, and finance firms directly, then investing in a variety of projects to create economic competition could noticeably affect market creation in the Middle East. On the other hand, once governments invest in a specific company or enterprise, they become responsible for ensuring that company succeeds and for staving off any attempts by local regimes to flounder it.

For real change to occur in the Middle East and to foster freer economies, support must come from the international community for private-sector creation and the promotion of businesses outside government control. True competition and the emergence of a private sector are no longer luxuries but necessary to create jobs for an evermore connected and worldly youth. Economic and financial literacy should be integrated into primary education. In turn, the return of the middle class depends on these countries' ability to meet the rising demand for honorable work.

In addition to the invisible hand, there is the state. Limiting extensive state intrusion in the economy need not mean no state involvement. Effective, transparent, and law-bound state institutions can drive growth. Saudi Arabia's Ma'aden and Sabic are good examples of state-owned enterprises that have evolved into successful multinational corporations. In the UAE, state ownership through diverse investment vehicles has not stifled competition.[93]

Outside of external intervention and support, Arab countries have already begun to initiate internal reforms. The UAE has already undertaken some of these measures by promoting a burgeoning tech finance industry that encourages companies such as Jamalon, a Jordan-based bookselling website, to link up with Dubai operations offices to promote business.[94]

Technology is now more accessible than ever to lower echelons of society, allowing some degree of economic mobility where social mobility is lacking. For instance, Ala' Alsallal, the founder of Jamalon, was born in a Palestinian refugee camp and recently oversaw a $4 million company expansion.[95]

One move the Emirati government made to increase the potential for middle-class growth is passing a bankruptcy law. By allowing businesses to fail, the UAE is averting the possibility that businessmen would face jail time for penalties evoked surrounding debt and obligations. Due to this law and the capital available in Dubai, the UAE is spurring new growth in a middle class that might otherwise be floundering.

The economic performance of Middle East countries is all but uniform. The region juxtaposes Qatar, with the highest GDP per capita, and Yemen, one of the world's poorest countries. It is also prone to violent conflicts and vicious economic swings. Given such instability coupled with democratic deficit, economic prosperity of the citizenry is seldom the state's top priority.

Although many of the constraints on economic progress outlined above contributed to the Arab Spring uprisings, the urgent need to fix their economic policy remains lost on many Arab leaders. Regional cooperation remains elusive, even among the GCC countries. Country-specific economic reforms—such as tackling corruption, fixing the business climate to promote entrepreneurship, and closing the gender gap—make for more attainable goals that would also facilitate greater regional economic synergy. Moreover, the public would have greater agency if their demands were anchored on cleaner government and a level playing field rather than greater shares of government handouts, subsidies, and unproductive jobs.

Notes

1. Michael Ross, *The Oil Curse: How Petroleum Wealth Shapes the Development of Nations* (Princeton, NJ: Princeton University Press, 2013).

2. Richard Auty, "Oil and Development in the Middle East" (paper presented at the BRISMES Annual Conference on Revolution and Revolt: Understanding the Forms and Causes of Change, London, March 28, 2012), https://brismes2012.files.wordpress.com/2012/02/richard-auty-oil-and-development-in-the-middle-east.pdf.

3. Paul Collier, *The Bottom Billion: Why the Poorest Countries Are Failing and What Can Be Done About It* (New York: Oxford University Press, 2008).

4. Also, Macartan Humphreys, Jeffrey D. Sachs, and Joseph E. Stiglitz, eds., *Escaping the Resource Curse* (New York: Columbia University Press, 2007).

5. Ross, *The Oil Curse*.

6. Ross, *The Oil Curse*.

7. US Energy Information Administration, "Short-Term Energy Outlook," July 9, 2019, https://www.eia.gov/outlooks/steo/report/prices.php.

8. Jeff D. Colgan, *Petro-Aggression: When Oil Causes War* (New York: Cambridge University Press, 2013).

9. *Economist*, "The End of the Oil Age," October 23, 2003, https://www.economist.com/node/2155717.

10. World Bank, "How Is Saudi Arabia Reacting to Low Oil Prices?," July 18, 2016, http://www.worldbank.org/en/country/gcc/publication/economic-brief-july-saudi-arabia-2016.

11. Ross, *The Oil Curse*.

12. Transparency International, "50 Million People in the Middle East and North Africa Paid Bribes Last Year," May 3, 2016, https://www.transparency.org/news/feture/50_million_people_in_the_middle_east_and_north_africa_paid_bribes_last_year.

13. Coralie Pring, "Iraq: Overview of Corruption and Anti-Corruption," Transparency International, July 5, 2015, https://knowledgehub.transparency.org/helpdesk/iraq-overview-of-corruption-and-anti-corruption.

14. Marwa Fatafta, "Rampant Corruption in Arab States," Transparency International, February 21, 2018, https://www.transparency.org/news/feature/rampant_corruption_in_arab_states.

15. Transparency International, "Aman Launches No to Wasta and Impunity Campaigns," November 14, 2003, https://www.transparency.org/news/pressrelease/AMAN_no_impunity_no_wasta_campaign_in_palestine.

16. Transparency International, "Corruption in the MENA Region" (working paper, Berlin, Germany, February 1, 2009), https://www.transparency.org/whatwedo/publication/working_paper_no._02_2009_corruption_in_the_mena_region.

17. Middle East and North Africa–Organisation for Economic Co-operation and Development Investment Programme, "Business Ethics and Anti-Bribery Policies in Selected Middle East and North African Countries," http://www.oecd.org/mena/competitiveness//36086689.pdf.

18. ForeignAssistance.gov, "Humanitarian Assistance," https://foreignassistance.gov/

categories/Humanitarian-Assistance. Also, see US Agency for International Development, "USAID History," May 7, 2019, https://www.usaid.gov/who-we-are/usaid-history.

19. Jeremy M. Sharp and Carla E. Humud, "U.S. Foreign Assistance to the Middle East: Historical Background, Recent Trends, and the FY2016 Request," Congressional Research Service, October 19, 2015, https://fas.org/sgp/crs/mideast/R44233.pdf.

20. Hilton L. Root, *Alliance Curse: How America Lost the Third World* (Washington, DC: Brookings Institution Press, 2008).

21. Root, *Alliance Curse.*

22. Millennium Challenge Corporation, "About MMC," https://www.mcc.gov/about.

23. Geoffrey Kemp, *The East Moves West: India, China, and Asia's Growing Presence in the Middle East* (Washington, DC: Brookings Institution Press, 2010), 3–21.

24. International Labour Organization, "Labour Migration," http://www.ilo.org/beirut/areasofwork/labour-migration/lang--en/index.htm.

25. Froilan T. Malit Jr. and Ali Al Youha, "Labor Migration in the United Arab Emirates: Challenges and Responses," Migration Policy Institute, September 18, 2013, https://www.migrationpolicy.org/article/labor-migration-united-arab-emirates-challenges-and-responses.

26. Malit and Youha, "Labor Migration in the United Arab Emirates."

27. Omar Al Ubaydli, "Economics 101: Should Arabian Gulf Countries Worry About Remittances?," *National*, October 7, 2017, https://www.thenational.ae/business/economics-101-should-arabian-gulf-countries-worry-about-remittances-1.665018.

28. Dilip Ratha, Sonia Plaza, and Ervin Dervisevic, *Migration and Remittances Factbook 2016: Third Edition*, World Bank Group, 2016, https://siteresources.worldbank.org/INTPROSPECTS/Resources/334934-1199807908806/4549025-1450455807487/Factbookpart1.pdf.

29. Ratha, Plaza, and Dervisevic, *Migration and Remittances Factbook 2016.*

30. World Bank, "Personal Remittances, Received (% of GDP)," 2019, https://data.worldbank.org/indicator/BX.TRF.PWKR.DT.GD.ZS?name_desc=false.

31. O. Rahmouni and I. Debbiche, "The Effects of Remittances Outflows on Economic Growth in Saudi Arabia: Empirical Evidence," *Journal of Economics and International Finance* 9, no. 5 (May 2017): 36–43, https://www.academicjournals.org/journal/JEIF/article-full-text-pdf/1BBBD4464406; and Central Bank of Bangladesh, "Monthly Data of Wages Earner's Remittance," July 2016, https://www.bb.org.bd/econdata/wageremitance.php.

32. Ross, *The Oil Curse.*

33. Ahmed Farouk Ghoneim, "Egypt and Subsidies: A Country Living Beyond Its Means," Middle East Institute, May 5, 2014, http://www.mei.edu/content/egypt-and-subsidies-country-living-beyond-its-means.

34. World Bank, "Government Expenditure on Education, Total (% of GDP)," https://data.worldbank.org/indicator/SE.XPD.TOTL.GD.ZS?locations=EG&view=chart; and Oxford Business Group, "Egypt Increases Spending on Education and Improves Quality and Access," https://oxfordbusinessgroup.com/overview/focus-point-increase-spending-should-support-aim-improving-quality-well-access.

35. World Bank, "Government Expenditure on Education, Total (% of GDP)."

36. World Bank, "Subsidies and Other Transfers (% of Expense)," https://data.

worldbank.org/indicator/GC.XPN.TRFT.ZS?end=2015&locations=EG-1A&start=1987.

37. Ross, *The Oil Curse*.

38. International Monetary Fund, *If Not Now, When? Energy Price Reform in Arab Countries*, April 2017, https://www.imf.org/en/Publications/Policy-Papers/Issues/2017/06/13/if-not-now-when-energy-price-reform-in-arab-countries.

39. Ross, *The Oil Curse*.

40. According to a report by Bank of America Merrill Lynch, in 2011, GCC governments spent an extra $150 billion on social projects such as housing, schools, and hospitals to stave off public discontent. Elizabeth Broomhall, "Arab Spring Has Cost Gulf Arab States $150bn," *Arabian Business*, September 8, 2011, http://www.arabianbusiness.com/arab-spring-has-cost-gulf-arab-states-150bn-419429.html; and Neil MacFarquhar, "In Saudi Arabia, Royal Funds Buy Peace for Now," *New York Times*, June 8, 2011, https://www.nytimes.com/2011/06/09/world/middleeast/09saudi.html.

41. Ross, *The Oil Curse*.

42. Ross, *The Oil Curse*.

43. Krista Mahr, "Bread Is Life: Food and Protest in Egypt," *Time*, January 31, 2011, http://science.time.com/2011/01/31/bread-is-life-food-and-protest-in-egypt/.

44. Wael Mahdi and Vivian Nereim, "Saudi Arabia Delays Energy-Subsidy Cuts," *Bloomberg*, July 6, 2017, https://www.bloomberg.com/news/articles/2017-07-06/saudis-are-said-to-delay-energy-subsidy-cuts-amid-economic-pain.

45. Ehab Farouk, "Egypt to Cut Fuel Subsidies as Government Seeks to Reduce Deficit," *Reuters*, April 9, 2016, https://www.reuters.com/article/us-egypt-budget-subsidies-idUSKCN0X60EB.

46. Norman Myers, "Lifting the Veil on Perverse Subsidies," *Nature: International Journal of Science* 392, no. 1 (1998): 327–28, http://www.nature.com/nature/journal/v392/n6674/abs/392327a0.html. Also, see Benedict Clements et al., *Energy Subsidy Reform: Lessons and Implications* (New York: International Monetary Fund, 2013).

47. International Monetary Fund, *If Not Now, When?*

48. Todd Moss, Caroline Lambert, and Stephanie Majerowicz, *Oil to Cash: Fighting the Resource Curse Through Cash Transfers* (Washington, DC: Brookings Institution Press, 2015).

49. International Monetary Fund, *If Not Now, When?*

50. Ghoneim, "Egypt and Subsidies."

51. Daron Acemoglu and James A. Robinson, *Why Nations Fail: The Origins of Power, Prosperity, and Poverty* (New York: Crown Business, 2012).

52. Hafez Ghanem, "Arab Countries in Transition: Support Inclusive Institutions," Brookings Institution, May 12, 2014, https://www.brookings.edu/opinions/arab-countries-in-transition-support-inclusive-institutions/.

53. Andrew England and Heba Saleh, "How the Middle East Is Sowing Seeds of a Second Arab Spring," *Financial Times*, March 5, 2018, https://www.ft.com/content/a6229844-1ad3-11e8-aaca-4574d7dabfb6.

54. England and Saleh, "How the Middle East Is Sowing Seeds of a Second Arab Spring."

55. Triska Hamid, "Corruption and Cronyism Hinder Kurdistan," *Financial Times*, September 5, 2012, https://www.ft.com/content/ea716668-f759-11e1-8c9d-00144fabdc0.

56. Tatyana Stanovaya, "Rotating the Elite: The Kremlin's New Personnel Policy,"

Carnegie Endowment for International Peace, January 30, 2018, http://carnegie.ru/2018/01/30/rotating-elite-kremlin-s-new-personnel-policy-pub-75379; and Denise Natali, "Coddling Iraqi Kurds," *Foreign Policy*, April 4, 2012, http://foreignpolicy.com/2012/04/04/coddling-iraqi-kurds/.

57. The *Guardian* once described Russian oligarchs as "about as popular with your average Russian as a man idly burning bundles of £50s outside an orphanage." Andrew Mueller, "What a Carve-Up!," *Guardian*, December 2, 2005, https://www.theguardian.com/media/2005/dec/03/tvandradio.russia.

58. Melani Cammett et al., *A Political Economy of the Middle East* (New York: Avalon Publishing, 2015), 29–31.

59. Ibrahim Saif, "The Middle Class and Transformations in the Arab World," Carnegie Endowment for International Peace, November 2, 2011, https://carnegie-mec.org/2011/11/02/middle-class-and-transformations-in-arab-world-pub-45895.

60. Saif, "The Middle Class and Transformations in the Arab World."

61. Elena Ianchovichina, *Eruptions of Popular Anger: The Economics of the Arab Spring and Its Aftermath*, World Bank Group, 2018, http://documents.worldbank.org/curated/en/251971512654536291/pdf/121942-REVISED-Eruptions-of-Popular-Anger-preliminary-rev.pdf.

62. Lida Bteddini, "Governance and Public Sector Employment in the Middle East and North Africa," World Bank, September 5, 2012, http://blogs.worldbank.org/arab-voices/governance-and-public-sector-employment-middle-east-and-north-africa.

63. Sylvia Smith, "Saudi Arabia's New Desert Megacity," BBC News, March 20, 2015, http://www.bbc.com/news/world-middle-east-31867727.

64. Steve Crabtree, "Two-Thirds of Young Arab Women Remain out of Workforce," Gallup, April 2, 2012, http://www.gallup.com/poll/153659/two-thirds-young-arab-women-remain-workforce.aspx.

65. World Bank, *Jobs for Shared Prosperity: Time for Action in the Middle East and North Africa*, April 12, 2013, http://documents.worldbank.org/curated/en/540401468051871415/Full-report.

66. Gallup, "2018 Global Great Jobs Briefing," 2018, https://news.gallup.com/reports/233375/gallup-global-great-jobs-report-2018.aspx.

67. World Bank Group, *World Development Report 2012: Gender Equality and Development*, 2012, https://openknowledge.worldbank.org/handle/10986/4391.

68. World Economic Forum, "The Global Gender Gap Report 2018," 2018, http://www3.weforum.org/docs/WEF_GGGR_2018.pdf.

69. UN Development Programme, *Arab Human Development Report 2016: Youth and the Prospects for Human Development in a Changing Reality*, 2016, http://www.arab-hdr.org/reports/2016/english/AHDR2016En.pdf.

70. UN Development Programme, *Arab Human Development Report 2016*.

71. Ross, *The Oil Curse*.

72. Shuchita Kapur, "UAE Retirement Age Set to Go up by One Year from February-End," Emirates 24/7, February 24, 2016, http://www.emirates247.com/news/uae-retirement-age-set-to-go-up-by-one-year-from-february-end-2016-02-24-1.622044.

73. World Bank, "Women in Jordan—Limited Economic Participation and Continued Inequality," April 17, 2014, http://www.worldbank.org/en/news/feature/2014/04/17/

women-in-jordan---limited-economic-participation-and-continued-inequality.

74. *Wall Street Journal*, "Saudi Women and Bill Gates," January 27, 2007, https://blogs.wsj.com/davos/2007/01/27/saudi-women-and-bill-gates/.

75. Seymour Martin Lipset, "Some Social Requisites of Democracy: Economic Development and Political Legitimacy," *American Political Science Review* 53, no. 1 (March 1959): 69–105, https://scholar.harvard.edu/files/levitsky/files/lipset_1959.pdf; and Samuel P. Huntington, *The Third Wave: Democratization in the Late Twentieth Century* (Norman, OK: University of Oklahoma Press, 1991).

76. Cammett et al., *A Political Economy of the Middle East*, 415.

77. Robert Booth, "Qatar World Cup Construction 'Will Leave 4,000 Migrant Workers Dead,'" *Guardian*, September 26, 2013, https://www.theguardian.com/global-development/2013/sep/26/qatar-world-cup-migrant-workers-dead.

78. Nobel Prize, "The Nobel Peace Prize for 2015," press release, October 10, 2015, https://www.nobelprize.org/nobel_prizes/peace/laureates/2015/press.html.

79. Ibrahim Al-A-Af, "Taarikh Al-Haraka Al-Ummaliya fi Al-Iraq" [History of the labor movement in Iraq], *Almada Supplements*, April 28, 2013, http://almadasupplements.com/news.php?action=view&id=7378#sthash.bujIsRJ6.dpbs.

80. Azzaman, "Tatawir Al-Tandhimat Al-Naqabiya fi Al-Iraq" [The development of syndicates in Iraq], August 17, 2014, https://www.azzaman.com/تطور-التنظيمات-النقابية-في-العراق/.

81. Aref Mohammed, "Iraq's Weakened Unions Fight Foreign Oil Firms," Reuters, July 13, 2009, https://www.reuters.com/article/us-iraq-oil-workers-sb/iraqs-weakened-unions-fight-foreign-oil-firms-idUSTRE56C2NM20090713.

82. At the Iraq Energy Forum on March 28, 2018, Salem Chalabi, partner at Stephenson Harwood Middle East LLP, relayed a story about how the Iraqi government canceled a joint venture with a foreign dairy firm that sought to increase the output of an Iraqi state-owned factory by a factor of eight using modern technology. But the new factory would need only three operators. The government canceled the deal to avoid angering the 200 workers at the plant. Iraq imported more than $900 million of dairy product in 2016. Michael Hussey, "Iraq Dairy Market," Bord Bia, February 9, 2018, https://www.borbia.ie/industry/manufacturers/insight/alerts/pages/iraqdairymarket.aspx.

83. Wamda, *Understanding the Arab Digital Generation*, October 10, 2012, https://www.wamda.com/2012/10/understanding-the-arab-digital-generation-report.

84. Tarek Elmasry et al., *Digital Middle East: Transforming the Region into a Leading Digital Economy*, McKinsey & Company, October 2016, https://www.mckinsey.com/~/media/mckinsey/global%20themes/middle%20east%20and%20africa/digital%20middle%20east%20transforming%20the%20region%20into%20a%20leading%20digital%20economy/digital-middle-east-final-updated.ashx.

85. Elmasry et al., *Digital Middle East*.

86. Wamda, *Understanding the Arab Digital Generation*.

87. Atlantic Council, *Economic Recovery and Revitalization*, February 2016, https://www.atlanticcouncil.org/images/publications/Economic_Recovery_and_Revitalization_Report_0203_web.pdf.

88. Maysa Jalbout and Samar Farah, *Will the Technology Disruption Widen or Close the*

Skills Gap in the Middle East and North Africa?, Brookings Institution, March 2016, https://www.brookings.edu/wp-content/uploads/2016/07/Technology-Disruptionv5.pdf.

89. Jalbout and Farah, *Will the Technology Disruption Widen or Close the Skills Gap in the Middle East and North Africa?*

90. Elmasry et al., *Digital Middle East.*

91. Wamda, http://www.wamda.com/; and UN Development Programme, *Arab Human Development Report 2016*, 85.

92. International Finance Corporation, https://www.ifc.org/wps/wcm/connect/corp_ext_content/ifc_external_corporate_site/home.

93. Alissa Amico, "The 'Invisible Hand' of the State in MENA Economies," *Washington Post*, March 4, 2015, https://www.washingtonpost.com/news/monkey-cage/wp/2015/03/04/the-limits-of-privatization-in-the-middle-east/.

94. Christopher M. Schroeder, "A Different Story from the Middle East: Entrepreneurs Building an Arab Tech Economy," *MIT Technology Review*, August 3, 2017, https://www.technologyreview.com/s/608468/a-different-story-from-the-middle-east-entrepreneurs-building-an-arab-tech-economy/.

95. Schroeder, "A Different Story from the Middle East."

7

What Reforms Do Good Governance Require?

BRIAN KATULIS

The 2011 Arab uprisings and their aftermath should have served as a
wake-up call on the need for good governance. In hindsight, the
writing was on the wall. For more than 15 years before the unrest, the
International Monetary Fund (IMF) and the World Bank reported that
most countries in the region had failed to initiate the deep governance
reforms needed to respond to overwhelming economic, social, political,
and demographic challenges.[1] Beginning in 2002 and for the next several
years, the United Nations Development Programme published a series of
Arab Human Development Reports written by Arab intellectuals that also
warned about the growing challenges facing Arab societies.[2]

In the wake of the Arab uprisings, countries across the region
engaged in different governance experiments: Tunisia chose democracy, Egypt embraced authoritarianism coupled with technocratic economic reforms, and monarchies like Saudi Arabia adopted top-down
reform influenced by management consulting. In addition, new governance emerged at the subnational level in Iraq, Libya, Syria, and Yemen.

"Governance" is a term that has many different meanings and aspects,
but the World Bank offers one standard definition: "the manner in
which power is exercised in the management of a country's economic
and social resources for development."[3] There are several key aspects
of governance, including how governments are selected, monitored,
and replaced and the capacity of a government to effectively formu-
late and implement sound policies. Governance also includes budget-
ing, taxation, administrative reform, the rule of law, the performance
of justice institutions, and management of public resources.

Governance has challenged leaders in the region for decades. Whether
countries are governing capably contributes to overall stability in the

Middle East and North Africa. Governance has become particularly relevant in recent debates in conflict and post-conflict environments such as Iraq, Libya, Syria, and Yemen—where the questions of who governs, how they come to power, and whether they have popular legitimacy are each viewed as essential ingredients to stability. The United States has spent years and hundreds of billions of dollars seeking to foster better governance in conflict and post-conflict environments, but these efforts have yet to produce sustainable results.[4]

In the wake of the Arab uprisings, three main categories of governance experimentation have emerged: republics that have experimented in governance after leadership change and political turbulence, fragmented countries that have experimented with new forms of decentralized and local governance, and preemptive top-down reform among monarchies.

Can Republics Reform?

Republics such as Egypt and Tunisia and were the first countries to experience political turbulence and leadership changes. Tunisia's reformed political system has yet to prove capable of executing substantive policy changes, while Egypt has yet to fundamentally reform its basic political and economic system.[5] Iraq, in contrast, had its system rebuilt almost from scratch in the wake of Saddam Hussein's 2003 ouster. Even there, however, the process is far from complete.

Part of the reason for stalled transition is the realities each country faces. Since 2011, Egyptian leaders have focused much of their time and efforts on immediate economic challenges and structural reforms. The 2013 ouster of democratically elected President Mohamed Morsi and the Muslim Brotherhood–led government brought Gen. Abdel Fattah el-Sisi to power and ushered in a new era of harsh political repression, which closed off the space for basic freedoms that existed under previous regimes.

At the same time, the 2013 ouster also introduced a set of new ideas, especially in economic policy, that have produced some incremental reform, such as implementing a value-added tax, adding a SmartCard system for food subsidies, and rolling back energy subsidies. The August 2017 passage of a new law that incentivized foreign investment also generated

results. These reforms and the accompanying multibillion-dollar injec-
tion of international capital appear to have paid off with faster economic
growth, lower unemployment rates, and stabilized inflation.[6]

Still, the Egyptian economy remains heavily dependent on external
assistance. Sisi's megaprojects—a second Suez Canal and a new capital—
have only reinforced Egypt's traditional economic policy approach. No real
measures have been taken to unravel the dominant roles the military and
state play in the economy.

Noneconomic reforms remain largely unimplemented. Reform efforts
have yet to produce a major shift in the courts, police, and other service
provisions. Despite the 2014 constitutional mandate to decentralize and
the Egyptian government's talk about moving to empower regional and
local authorities, authorities in Cairo continue to monopolize all meaningful decisions. Recent studies have found that Egypt remains one of the
most centralized countries in the world, ranking 114 of 158.[7]

Articles 175–183 of Egypt's latest constitution set out a framework for
establishing local councils with independent budgets financed through revenues from locally generated taxes. Nevertheless, other provisions in the
constitution appear to limit the prospective authority and power of local
councils to operate independently, including giving authority to centrally
appointed executive authorities to interfere with local council decisions.

But the support for decentralized governance remains unclear for the
broader Egyptian public, and several Egyptian analysts remain skeptical
that a new opening for local governance will materialize. "Decentralization
is against the culture and logic of Egypt's hierarchical society," one analyst
indicated in an interview in Cairo. "The executive branch always has the
upper hand, and a key part of the challenge is resistance from the central
government to give up control over the budget and funding decisions at
all levels."[8]

Recent IMF-backed reforms have not challenged Egypt's existing governance model. Domestic stability drives the current government's policy,
and IMF-backed reforms are best seen as a way to preserve that stability.
They are unlikely to provide the impetus for wide-ranging and far-reaching
changes to Egyptian governance.

For all its faults in delivering prosperity or accountability, this model
of a military- and state-dominated economy presided over by a repressive

government with nominal elections has been resilient. It has survived shifts in policy and substantial reforms without change to its core components. Historically, liberalizing reforms have led to better national economic performance without improving or even significantly altering Egyptian governance as a whole.

In contrast, Iraq's model of governance has seen substantial changes in recent years, with leaders demonstrating an openness to continue reforming how the country is governed out of practical necessity. "We don't have a choice but to decentralize," one senior Iraqi leader told a closed forum in Washington, DC, while also acknowledging that the Iraqi public views the central government as more efficient than regional and local governments.[9] Iraq still faces substantial challenges in governance, including endemic corruption, a dearth of qualified personnel to serve at various levels of government, and continued political deadlock that impedes decision-making and policy implementation.

After the 2011 withdrawal of American troops from the country, the limitations of Iraq's post-Saddam governance model became more apparent. Prime Minister Nouri al-Maliki's government hollowed out the Iraqi military and alienated much of Iraq's Sunni Arab population, paving the way for the Islamic State's 2014 seizure of Mosul and other broad swathes of territory.[10] Maliki's successor, Haider al-Abadi, had success rebuilding the Iraqi military with the help of the American-led counter-ISIS coalition. But the success of Muqtada al-Sadr's political bloc in Iraq's 2018 parliamentary elections and subsequent anti-government protests across the country demonstrated that military success against the Islamic State would not get Abadi far enough politically in the face of Iraq's continuing governance problems.[11]

Democracy and elections have not solved the governance problems that emerged in Iraq after the removal of Saddam Hussein. Indeed, Iraq's elections likely contributed to these problems by elevating corrupt sectarian actors like Maliki and, in his previous guise, Sadr to influential and powerful political positions. Although Sadr has since positioned himself as a reformer and taken advantage of popular dissatisfaction with Iraqi governance, as in Egypt, there appears to be little appetite for substantive improvement in governance that would hurt the power and influence of Iraq's existing political parties and movements.

Can Fragmentation Bolster Local Governance?

The wave of political unrest that swept through the region in 2011 may have caused governments in Libya, Syria, and Yemen to fragment, but, in reality, the problem of state fragmentation long predates the so-called Arab Spring. A broad range of exceptional circumstances fragmented and divided countries and territories such as Lebanon, the West Bank, and the Gaza Strip—where terrorist actors like Hezbollah and Hamas effectively run their own private states—enabling the rise of non-state actors to play an influential role in governance.

Poor governance and power struggles—sometimes purely political and sometimes along ethnic and sectarian lines—each contributed to state collapse in Libya, Syria, and Yemen. As the central government lost control, different models of governance emerged at the local levels in each state, from Kurdish federalism to the Islamic State in Syria and Iraq. In no case, however, did any stable system of governance emerge—nor is one likely to emerge in the short term.

The Islamic State did propose and implement an alternative model of governance by force. Its brutal approach to law and order and focused management of property contracts, land, and energy enabled the group to develop a temporary grip on power in parts of Syria and Iraq. During its more than three years in power, the Islamic State created a system of governance based on brutal coercion rather than the day-to-day provision of public services. Although characterized in some cases as "more capable than the government it had replaced" in Iraq and possessing the trappings of bureaucracy, more often than not the Islamic State simply took over existing state institutions and repurposed them to its own ends.[12]

In effect, the Islamic State mounted a hostile takeover of state institutions in the territory it conquered.[13] As one resident of Mosul later told the *New York Times*, "We had no choice but to go back to work. We did the same job as before. Except we were now serving a terrorist group."[14]

These state institutions were repurposed to suit the Islamic State's goals and methods. Mosul's Directorate of Agriculture, for instance, became the Islamic State's Ministry of Agriculture and handled the group's confiscation of land owned by evicted religious minorities.[15] These improved efficiencies in governance under the Islamic State—such as faster processing of land-rent applications by the Mosul agriculture department—can be attributed to the Islamic State's constant need for revenue as much as any inherent propensity for good governance.

Still, public services provided by the Islamic State were irregular and inconsistent. In Mosul, for example, the group failed to sustain the electricity supply and struggled with trash collection and water supply.[16] Even in its capital Raqqa, where its services, hospitals, and schools were most developed, the Islamic State failed to keep the lights on.[17]

For the Islamic State, governance had two primary definitions: enforcing its own millenarian religious ideology on local populations and waging an ongoing military campaign to expand and defend its territory. In addition to coercion, the Islamic State used tax policy as a way to carry out its ideological vision. Shi'ites and non-Muslims, for instance, were required to pay a tax of up to $2,500 a year to continue living in the Islamic State's territory.[18] It redistributed confiscated property of religious minorities to Islamic State supporters, including foreign fighters and their relatives.[19] Fines for proscribed behavior like cigarette smoking ($25) or a woman showing her eyes ($10) both imposed the Islamic State's religious ideology and raised money to pay for fighters who accounted for as much as half the budget.[20]

The Islamic State was not the only group seeking to build a new government or system upon the fragmentation of Syrian state rule. In northeastern Syria, even before receiving US air support and other supplies, the Democratic Union Party (*Partiya Yekîtiya Demokrat*, PYD) assumed management of areas Syrian President Bashar al-Assad abandoned or wrested from his Islamist opponents. Today, the PYD controls much of northeastern Syria. Ideologically, the PYD adheres to the form of decentralized, stateless socialist governance espoused by incarcerated Kurdistan Workers Party (*Partiya Karkerên Kurdistanê*, PKK) leader and theoretician Abdullah Öcalan. According to this ideology, elected local councils provide the foundation for governance up to the level of the Democratic Autonomous Administration that runs the three cantons—each with their own governments, legislatures, and judicial systems—that constitute the Autonomous Administration of North and East Syria.[21]

In practice, however, this utopian political project serves as ideological cover for continued PYD control over northeastern Syria. The

PYD-dominated Movement for a Democratic Society (*Tevgera Civaka Demokratîk*, TEV-DEM) coalition leads a murky process of "coordination" between Rojava's cantons and denies holding power but nevertheless "leads society."[22] Like other political movements and parties promoting stateless systems of governance, the PYD holds and exercises de facto state power while formally disavowing it. Accordingly, the 3,000-plus local communes established by the PYD in northeastern Syria function more as administrative bodies than political institutions, providing basic services such as food and fuel while serving as a conduit to the real but informal PYD political authorities. Indeed, TEV-DEM still retained budgetary authority over the communes as of early 2018.[23]

That said, the PYD produced some results in certain areas of governance as it consolidated control over territory the Islamic State seized. The People's Protection Units (*Yekîneyên Parastina Gel*, YPG), the party's militia, has effectively fought against the Islamic State. It provides basic services to local populations under its authority and has built schools and even universities, all of which help the PYD consolidate power.[24] Most notably, the PYD has made significant strides in integrating women into key components of local governance such as the police and judiciary—even in conservative, largely Arab areas like Manbij.[25]

Still, PYD legitimacy in northeastern Syria remains fragile and limited, in no small part due to concerns about its methods of governance. Although concerns about exclusion along ethnic lines remain prevalent, broader concerns transcend divisions between Kurds and Arabs. As one Syrian activist explained, "They [the PYD] don't tolerate any type of dissent—Arab or Kurdish."[26] This intolerance of dissent suggests fragility: Without informed consent and popular legitimacy, efforts to administer local governance may face the same challenges that have plagued Syria for decades.

While the PYD and its supporters in Europe and the United States claim that Rojava represents a new and revolutionary model of governance, in practice, the PYD follows a model of governance similar to other political groups with utopian aspirations of statelessness. Although it has accomplished much in areas like service provision, the PYD's formal commitment to decentralized governance masks its informal dominance over northeastern Syria. The disconnect between the PYD's formal institutions and the group's informal power increases the likelihood that its governance project will drift in an authoritarian direction.

More broadly, the long-term challenge in a fragmented country like Syria is how ongoing conflicts in the country will be resolved, how power will be consolidated, and how the pathway for producing a system of governance at the local, regional, and national levels that is responsive to citizens' concerns will be created. For the time being, it appears Syria will de facto have multiple models of governance inside its borders, and one key issue for stability is how these models will be mediated and synchronized in a future Syrian state. The likelihood of a decentralized federal system of government appears strong.

In Lebanon, Hezbollah, the political organization and terrorist group, has operated in the confines of the Lebanese government's formal structures while also building its own quasi-state structures, including a separate paramilitary organization and charitable organizations. In the Gaza Strip, the terrorist group Hamas has wielded control of formal governance structures since 2007, when it seized control by force from the Palestinian National Authority. Both examples of governance—Hezbollah and Hamas—serve as dysfunctional examples in which a weak or nonexistent state is dominated by a subnational force lacking broad legitimacy.

Can Monarchies Survive?

The most innovative and promising experiments in governance reforms are found in the oil-rich Gulf countries such as the United Arab Emirates and, in particular, Saudi Arabia. Monarchies have introduced governance reforms largely because they have additional resources and capacity to do so. However, they have not embraced a single formula.

Saudi Arabia's Vision 2030—a major plan to diversify the Saudi economy; reduce the country's dependence on oil revenues; reform a wide range of public services including education, health, and infrastructure; and introduce tougher measures to counter corruption—is the most prominent reform plan in the region.[27] Introduced in early 2016, the broad vision seeks to rewrite the social contract, which has been at the core of the kingdom since its establishment, to transform Saudi Arabia from a bloated welfare state to a new model that imbues citizens with greater responsibilities, including paying taxes for service provision. Other measures include cutting the public sector, reducing the religious establishment's influence on many aspects of governance, and increasing consultations with the public.[28]

The imperative to rewrite the social contract is born out of the recognition that the Saudi political economy model is not sustainable. "We had a young population. And we were providing for the population, you know subsidized energy, subsidized water, subsidized medicine, subsidized education, we subsidized everybody's life . . . and no taxes," argued Mohammed Al-Shaikh, a key figure in the economic reform efforts, a minister of state, and a member of the Council of Economic and Development Affairs.[29] Saudi Arabia's government is moving to reduce subsidies and increase the burden paid by Saudis to rewrite the social contract.

An important component of Vision 2030 is an effort to restructure governance inside the kingdom. Shortly after the release of the plan, the Saudi Council of Ministers issued the National Transformation Program, which outlined Vision 2030's implementation.[30] The Saudi Council of Ministers tasked the Council of Economic and Development Affairs to create a system to monitor and evaluate the implementation of changes in 24 government bodies with interim targets for 2020. In addition, the Saudi government established a number of bodies as part of the plan, including the National Center for Performance Measurement, the Delivery Unit, and the Project Management Office of the Council of Economic and Development Affairs.

The paradigms inherent in Western management and consulting firms heavily influenced the reformist plans, with a strong emphasis on key performance indicators for strategic objectives. This state-centric, bureaucratic approach to governance reform is an attempt to optimize the performance of sclerotic government agencies that have not faced tight scrutiny in the past.

One priority is to reduce the amount of money lost to corruption in all aspects of the country's governance, including public services, and to reduce the expense of the social safety net the kingdom has provided to its citizens for decades. One key figure involved in the Saudi reform effort highlighted the extent of the problem in a Riyadh interview: "The annual growth in money certain individuals were getting from energy corruption was higher than the country's gross domestic product growth and population growth."[31]

In many respects, Saudi Arabia lags behind its smaller neighbor, the United Arab Emirates, on the governance issue. More than a decade ago, the United Arab Emirates began introducing a number of measures aimed at enhancing governance with a focus on economic growth and promoting trade and investment. These governance reforms prioritized upgrading the efficiency of government ministries and expanding "free zones" to attract foreign direct investment with tax advantages for multinational corporations; the reforms did not seek to advance democratic reforms or fundamentally alter the monarchical system.[32] The United Arab Emirates operates as a federal system of seven emirates, and its focus in governance reform is on efficient service delivery.[33]

Another interesting development in governance between the two Gulf monarchies has been a recent move by Saudi Arabia and the United Arab Emirates to more closely synchronize their governance approach. In June 2018, the two countries announced a series of extensive agreements to implement a vision for economic, development, and military integration through 44 joint projects. Under the banner of the "Strategy of Resolve," the two countries set plans for joint efforts that directly shape how both will govern on a wide range of areas, including economic regulation, tax policy, public service provision, infrastructure, and financial technology.[34]

Beyond Saudi Arabia and the United Arab Emirates, other monarchies, including Bahrain, Jordan, Kuwait, Morocco, and Oman, lag behind in efforts to introduce new governance reforms. Jordan and Morocco have discussed decentralization efforts on governance for years, but these discussions have not yet altered the way the countries manage their resources for growth and development. Jordan has experienced recent turbulence related to economic reforms it introduced in spring 2018 aimed at reducing certain public subsidies to address the country's budget deficits and debt.

In Morocco, the monarchy attempted reforms that appear aimed at empowering more actors in government to assume greater authority and push decision-making away from the central government to regional and local actors. The views inside Morocco about these reform efforts are mixed.

Some argue that efforts have empowered more actors at various levels of government in Morocco. "Actors understand they must act—they don't wait for the king now," said one analyst with a leading think tank in discussing the reform process.[35] Others argue that regionalization and decentralization efforts are still in the early stages of implementation—and that the king and individuals close to him still wield a strong degree of power.

Unlike most of the Gulf monarchies, Jordan and Morocco have elected parliaments that play roles in debating policy priorities. In Morocco, one leader in parliament noted the long list of challenges facing the country, saying that "our national agenda is awash in competing priorities" and naming education as the number one challenge, followed by regionalization, devolution of power, and economic inequality.[36] As in Egypt, the actual implementation of devolution of authority to regional and local levels of government has remained slow and has lagged behind the expectations of many.

One common thread found in the monarchies of the Middle East and North Africa, both rich and poor, is placing a top priority on regime preservation. In a real sense, good governance in this context is a more efficient form of authoritarianism, one in which the avenues for policy formulation remain narrow.

How Will Governance Change in the Middle East and North Africa?

Anticipating the trends in governance in the broader region is difficult given the uncertainty that still exists in the region. But a mix of internal and external factors will likely shape and influence governance reform efforts and other governance experiments across the region. The 2011 Arab uprisings highlighted the danger of the status quo, but few countries have picked the lock on how to advance a good governance agenda.

In a sense, one challenge of governance is the chicken-and-egg dynamic as it relates to key issues such as education and health services. The quality of these public services largely remains low as a result of poor governance, but the low quality of education also prolongs the crisis in governance due to a dearth of talent and experience. Ironically, while many regimes recognize the need to reform to head off long-term unrest, instability elsewhere may be a disincentive to move from the rhetoric of reform to reality. Leaders will continue to present plans for major governance overhauls, but implementation will be slow. They are likely to prevent action that could unleash political forces that contribute to regime instability, undermine their own legitimacy, cut off patronage networks, and lead to their demise.

More broadly, the region suffers from poor governance in part because of the lack of public space and ordinary citizens' ability to shape and influence decision-making in many key parts of the region. This points to the broader political problems that remain at the core of instability in the region, including the unequal distribution of power within countries. All this translates into a tall agenda for countries in the region: conflict resolution in countries such as Libya, Syria, and Yemen that have fragmented due to conflict; a more inclusive model of governance that gives more authority and voice to regional and local levels of governance and respects the role of individuals to shape policy outcomes in places like Egypt; and a more sustained approach to introduce institutional reforms and make visions a reality in countries such as Saudi Arabia.

Good governance is an essential ingredient in building societies that are more resilient to multiple forces eating away at state structures across the region—terrorist movements like the Islamic State, revolutionary regional powers like Iran, and sectarianism. Absent significant reform, future youth-driven revolutions are a distinct prospect. More effective institutions that respond to the basic concerns and needs of citizens will not resolve the conflicts roiling many parts of the region, but well-functioning institutions stand a better chance of addressing the crushing economic, social, and demographic challenges facing the region.

Notes

1. International Monetary Fund, Middle East and Central Asia Department, "Regional Economic Outlook Update: Middle East, North Africa, Afghanistan, and Pakistan," May 18, 2018, 1–19, https://www.imf.org/en/Publications/REO/MECA/Issues/2018/04/24/mreo0518; and Lei Sandy Ye, "The Middle East and North Africa Outlook in Five Charts: Recovery After a Weak 2017," World Bank, January 30, 2018, https://blogs.worldbank.org/developmenttalk/middle-east-and-north-africa-outlook-five-charts-recovery-after-weak-2017.

2. UN Development Programme, Arab Fund for Economic and Social Development, *Arab Human Development Report 2002: Creating Opportunities for Future Generations*, 2002, http://hdr.undp.org/sites/default/files/rbas_ahdr2002_en.pdf.

3. World Bank, *Governance and Development*, April 1992, http://documents.worldbank.org/curated/en/604951468739447676/pdf/multi-page.pdf.

4. See, for example, Tamara Cofman Wittes, "Politics, Governance, and State-Society Relations," Atlantic Council, November 2016, http://www.atlanticcouncil.org/images/publications/Politics_Governance_and_State-Society_Relations_web_1121.pdf.

5. Saad Aldouri and Hamza Meddeb, "In Face of Protests, Tunisia Needs Bold Economic Reform," Chatham House, March 16, 2018, https://www.chathamhouse.org/expert/comment/face-protests-tunisia-needs-bold-economic-reforms.

6. International Monetary Fund, "Egypt: IMF Executive Board Completes Third Review Under the Extended Fund Facility," press release, July 2, 2018, https://www.imf.org/en/News/Articles/2018/07/02/pr18271-egypt-board-completes-3rd-review-under-eff.

7. Maksym Ivanyna and Anwar Shah, "How Close Is Your Government to Its People? Worldwide Indicators on Localization and Decentralization," *Economics: The Open-Access, Open-Assessment E-Journal* 8, no. 1 (Winter 2014): 1–61, http://dx.doi.org/10.5018/economics-ejournal.ja.2014-3.

8. Egyptian analyst, interview with the author, Cairo, Egypt, April 18, 2017.

9. Senior Iraqi leader, roundtable discussion, Washington, DC, March 22, 2017.

10. Zaid al-Ali, "How Maliki Ruined Iraq," *Foreign Policy*, June 19, 2014, https://foreignpolicy.com/2014/06/19/how-maliki-ruined-iraq/; James Jeffrey, "How Maliki Broke Iraq," *Politico*, August 13, 2014, https://www.politico.com/magazine/story/2014/08/how-maliki-broke-iraq-109996; and Greg Jaffe and Kevin Sullivan, "Collapse of Iraqi Army a Failure for Nation's Premier and for U.S. Military," *Washington Post*, June 12, 2014, https://www.washingtonpost.com/world/national-security/collapse-of-iraqi-army-a-failure-for-nations-premier-and-for-us-military/2014/06/12/25191bc0-f24f-11e3-914c-1fbd0614e2d4_story.html.

11. BBC News, "Basra Protests: Iraq Government Building Torched in New Unrest," September 6, 2018, https://www.bbc.com/news/world-middle-east-45441848; Margaret Coker, "Once Hated by U.S. and Tied to Iran, Is Sadr Now 'Face of Reform' in Iraq," *New York Times*, May 20, 2018, https://www.nytimes.com/2018/05/20/world/middleeast/iraq-election-sadr.html; and Deutsche-Welle, "Anti-Government Protests in Iraq Spread to Baghdad," July 22, 2018, https://www.dw.com/en/anti-government-protests-in-iraq-spread-to-baghdad/av-44776819.

12. Rukmini Callimanchi, "The ISIS Files," *New York Times*, April 4, 2018, https://www.nytimes.com/interactive/2018/04/04/world/middleeast/isis-documents-mosul-iraq.html.

13. Daniel Egel et al., *When the Islamic State Comes to Town: The Economic Impact of Islamic State Governance in Iraq and Syria*, RAND Corporation, 2017, 168, https://www.rand.org/nsrd/projects/when-isil-comes-to-town.html; and Callimanchi, "The ISIS Files."

14. Callimanchi, "The ISIS Files."

15. Callimanchi, "The ISIS Files."

16. Egel et al., *When the Islamic State Comes to Town*, 78–79.

17. Egel et al., *When the Islamic State Comes to Town*, 119.

18. Sarah Almukhtar, "Life Under the Islamic State: Fines, Taxes, and Punishments," *New York Times*, May 26, 2016, https://www.nytimes.com/interactive/2016/05/26/world/middleeast/isis-taxes-fines-revenue.html.

19. Callimanchi, "The ISIS Files."

20. Egel et al., *When the Islamic States Comes to Town*, 2.

21. Dan Wilkofsky, "The Commune System: A Look at Local PYD Governance in North Eastern Syria," Atlantic Council, March 12, 2018, http://www.atlanticcouncil.org/blogs/syriasource/the-commune-system-a-look-at-local-pyd-governance-in-northeastern-syria; Wes Enzinna, "A Dream of Secular Utopia in ISIS' Backyard," *New York Times*, November 24, 2015, https://www.nytimes.com/2015/11/29/magazine/a-dream-of-utopia-in-hell.html; and Rana Khalaf, "Governing Rojava: Layers of Legitimacy in Syria," Chatham House, December 2016, 5, 10–11, https://syria.chathamhouse.org/assets/documents/2016-12-08-governing-rojava-khalaf.pdf.

22. Khalaf, "Governing Rojava," 11.

23. Wilkosfsky, "The Commune System."

24. Khalaf, "Governing Rojava," 16–18.

25. Rod Nordland, "Women Are Free, and Armed, in Kurdish-Controlled Northern Syria," *New York Times*, February 24, 2018, https://www.nytimes.com/2018/02/24/world/middleeast/syria-kurds-womesns-rights-gender-equality.html.

26. Mona Yacoubian, "Governance Challenges in Raqqa After the Islamic State," United States Institute of Peace, 2017, 7, https://www.usip.org/sites/default/files/SR414-Governance-Challenges-in-Raqqa-after-the-Islamic-State.pdf.

27. Kingdom of Saudi Arabia, "Vision 2030," http://vision2030.gov.sa/en.

28. For a comprehensive assessment of Vision 2030 one year into its implementation, see Jane Kinninmont, *Vision 2030 and Saudi Arabia's Social Contract Austerity and Transformation*, Chatham House, July 2017, https://www.chathamhouse.org/sites/default/files/publications/research/2017-07-20-vision-2030-saudi-kinninmont.pdf.

29. Norah O'Donnell, "Saudi Arabia's Heir to the Throne Talks to 60 Minutes," *60 Minutes*, March 19, 2018, https://www.cbsnews.com/news/saudi-crown-prince-talks-to-60-minutes/.

30. Kingdom of Saudi Arabia, "National Transformation Program," http://vision2030.gov.sa/en/ntp.

31. Saudi Arabia reform key figure, interview with author, Riyadh, Saudi Arabia, February 19, 2017.

32. Jeremy Tamanini, "Development and Governance in the UAE, not Democracy," Carnegie Endowment for International Peace, August 19, 2008, http://carnegieendowment.org/sada/20887.

33. For more details, see UN Development Program, "United Arab Emirates: In-Depth," http://www.ae.undp.org/content/united_arab_emirates/en/home/ourwork/democraticgovernance/in_depth.html.

34. For more details on the plan, see Gulf News, "UAE, Saudi Arabia Announce Strategy of Resolve," June 7, 2018, https://gulfnews.com/news/uae/government/uae-saudi-arabia-announce-strategy-of-resolve-1.2233041.

35. Moroccan parliamentary leader, interview with author, Rabat, Morocco, May 2, 2017.

36. Senior official in Morocco's parliament, interview with author, Rabat, Morocco, May 4, 2017.

About the Authors

Thanassis Cambanis is a senior fellow at the Century Foundation, where he specializes in the Middle East and US foreign policy. He is a former foreign correspondent to the *Boston Globe* and contributor to the *New York Times*, *Foreign Policy*, and the *Atlantic*, among other publications.

Michael A. Fahy is an anthropologist and a lecturer at the University of Michigan School of Education. He is on the board of directors of the education nonprofit InGlobal, which focuses on instructional design and innovation, and a member of the University of Michigan's Interactive Communications and Simulations group.

Florence Gaub is the deputy director of the European Union Institute for Security Studies. She is the coauthor of *The Cauldron: NATO's Campaign in Libya* (Oxford University Press, 2018) and author of *Guardians of the Arab State: When Militaries Intervene in Politics, from Iraq to Mauritania* (Oxford University Press, 2017).

Brian Katulis is a senior fellow at the Center for American Progress, where he focuses on US national security strategy and counterterrorism policy. He is a veteran of the Bill Clinton administration's National Security Council, State Department, and Defense Department. He is also a senior adviser to the Albright Stonebridge Group, where he advises clients on issues pertaining to the Middle East and North Africa.

Danielle Pletka is the senior vice president of foreign and defense policy studies at the American Enterprise Institute, where she writes about national security issues in the Middle East. She also holds the Andrew H. Siegel Professorship on American Middle East Foreign Policy at Georgetown University's Walsh School of Foreign Service.

Michael Rubin is a resident scholar at the American Enterprise Institute, where he researches Arab and Iranian politics and society. He is the author of *Dancing with the Devil: The Perils of Engaging Rogue Regimes* (Encounter, 2014) and a former adviser in the Office of the Secretary of Defense.

Bilal Wahab is the Nathan and Esther K. Wagner Fellow at the Washington Institute for Near East Policy, where he focuses on governance in Kurdistan and economy. He has previously taught at the American University of Iraq, Sulaimani, where he founded the Center for Development and Natural Resources.

A. Kadir Yildirim is a fellow for the Middle East at Rice University's Baker Institute for Public Policy. He is the author of *Muslim Democratic Parties in the Middle East: Economy and Politics of Islamist Moderation* (Indiana University Press, 2016).

www.ingramcontent.com/pod-product-compliance
Lightning Source LLC
Chambersburg PA
CBHW062033270326
41929CB00014B/2420